P9-EEO-739

LIVING THE LIFE *YOU* WERE MEANT TO LIVE

TOM PATERSON

THOMAS NELSON PUBLISHERS
Nashville

Published in Nashville, Tennessee, by Thomas Nelson, Inc.

Library of Congress Cataloging-in-Publication Data

Paterson, Tom.
Living the life you were meant to live / Tom Paterson.
p. cm.
ISBN 0-7852-7195-3
1. Self-actualization (Psychology)—Religious aspects—Christianity. 2. Self-realization—Religious aspects—Christianity. 3. Christian life. I. Title.
BV4598.2.P38 1998
248.4—dc21 97–53278
CIP

Printed in the United States of America.

1 2 3 4 5 6 BVG 03 02 01 00 99 98

To

Ginny

My wonderful wife, the sunshine in my day,
my cheerleader for more than half a century.

God brought us together to make me whole.

He used you to teach me about love,
to release me through love to truly live.

I am His servant today because of you . . .
as He knew all along would be the result.

CONTENTS

FOREWORD

I first met Tom Paterson many years ago when our small group of local pastors asked him to spend a day with us and facilitate a discussion about how to better manage our growing churches. The day was so enjoyable and productive, we asked Tom back a second, a third, and even a fourth time. Tom's insights were invaluable to each of us. As a result of those sessions, Tom and I became great friends. Tom was one of the three strongest supporters, along with Peter Drucker and Bob Buford, of our *purpose-driven church* strategy in the formative years of Saddleback Church. When others said we were crazy, Tom encouraged me to stay on the path.

Years later, in 1993, the demands of a rapidly growing church and a full schedule of seminars caused me to feel overwhelmed and out of balance. Knowing Tom's organizational ability, I asked him to help me "organize" my personal life. I asked him to help me design a customized LifePlan that would balance my life and allow me to avoid the emotional burnout that is so common among executives and pastors. Tom agreed to help, and invited me to spend a couple of days with him at his and Ginny's beautiful mountain home, Whispering Pines. Together we looked at my strengths and weaknesses, sought God's will for my life, and then developed a strategy for fulfilling it. It was a wonderful, reaffirming experience, and I still rely on the insights I gained. In fact, the process of developing a LifePlan was so helpful to me that I paid for all my senior staff to go through a similar process during the next year.

Over twenty years ago I developed a little diagram, based on a baseball diamond, to visualize God's purpose for our lives and the process of spiritual growth. Today that Life Development Process is used in thousands of churches as a visual road map: (first base) *bringing people to Christ and into his church family,* (second base) *helping them grow to spiritual maturity,* (third base) *equipping them for ministry based on their unique "S.H.A.P.E.,"* and (home plate) *enabling them to share Christ and fulfill their life mission in the world.*

I believe that the process of LifePlanning is an essential tool for helping people get to home plate—that is, living the life in Christ that God means for each of us to live. Whenever churches help adults, teenagers, and even children discover the unique purpose that God made each of them for, then Christians are able to live the abundant life that Jesus talked about.

This is not the kind of book that you simply read and then place on your bookshelf. It is a process guide. Approach it prayerfully. Ask the Holy Spirit to be with you every step of the way. Take the time necessary to apply it to your life. Discover the truth, face the truth, and then act on the truth for God's glory. You will be amazed at what God can do with your life!

Dr. Rick Warren
Founding Pastor
Saddleback Valley Community Church
Mission Viejo, California

INTRODUCTION

As you read this book, you will encounter terms that you might not have seen before. They are used in a very specific way. You might find it helpful to refer to this page from time to time for the definitions of these terms.

LifePlan: The Lord had a plan for your life before your conception. He created you in a specific way—with a set of gifts, desires, and a certain "bent"—so that you might fulfill His plan for your life. Because this plan is God's plan and because God sees your life as a whole and undivided entity, the term *LifePlan* is written and capitalized in this way throughout the book.

A LifePlan is not something you construct but something you discover. God is the author; each of us is the recipient of a unique LifePlan.

LifePlanning: LifePlanning is the process of discovering God's plan for your life. The process involves the completion of a series of sequential exercises or modules intended to help you discover your uniqueness and the way in which God has been involved in every aspect of your life, all of your life.

Your unique giftedness points toward your unique purpose. In other words, God has given you gifts to use, and when you use your gifts, you fulfill your purpose in life. LifePlanning, therefore, is a process that primarily helps you discover your uniqueness.

For more than twenty years, I have conducted LifePlanning consultations. These are two- or three-day sessions with individual clients. During the consultations, I guide a person through the exercises found in this book to help the person gain perspective on his or her life. The terms *LifePlanning consultation* and *LifePlanning facilitation* refer to my work in helping others discover God's LifePlan for their lives.

At times in this book, I refer to "LifePlanning facilitators." These are people I have trained in recent years to conduct LifePlanning consultations.

The final stage of the LifePlanning process is the creation of a personal action plan that outlines specific steps to take *immediately* in response to the exercises that have been completed. This stage is unique to each person, is highly dependent on the answers generated by the exercises, and requires the person and a facilitator to engage in dialogue and prayer. Therefore, I could not include this stage in a book. There are simply too many directions you might take, too many variables in establishing what can and must be done immediately.

In most cases, however, action plans seem to write themselves. The decisions that need to be made and the direction that needs to be pursued become obvious in light of what a person has discovered in the LifePlanning exercises. It is my prayer that the Holy Spirit will help you determine your personal, highly individualized response to the material in this book. Allow the Holy Spirit to become your facilitator, leading you into a greater understanding of yourself and toward the steps that you need to take next in your life . . . truly to live *the life you were meant to live!*

For I know the thoughts that I think toward you, says the L*ORD*, *thoughts of peace and not of evil, to give you a future and a hope.*

—Jeremiah 29:11

1

A NEW LOOK AT YOUR LIFE AND FUTURE

Too many people are not living the life they are meant to live. God does not intend for this to happen. We are challenged to reverse this situation, not through using our own strength, but through yielding to God's desires.

Are you experiencing deep peace of soul today? Do you have a sure understanding about who you are and about God's plan and purpose for your life?

Do you have nagging, perhaps very deep-seated questions, such as, Where do I go from here? What does God have for me in the next phase of my life?

Is the Holy Spirit prompting you, Now is the time for a new work to begin in me or through me?

If these are your questions, this book is for you. God has a plan for your life. He will show you the path of life to take, and living in His presence you will find the "fullness of joy" (Ps. 16:11). I call this a LifePlan—God's plan for living the life you were meant to live.

Many people come to a LifePlan because they sense that life is out of balance in some way—they have a general feeling of uneasiness, inner conflict, or anxiety that something is not right.

Others come to a LifePlan because they face a period of transition in their lives—they recognize they are moving into a new phase, and they wonder how their purpose or function in life might change.

Still others come to the LifePlanning process because they sense that something could be better or that something needs to be added to their lives in order for them to feel a greater sense of purpose and meaning.

People rarely come for casual reasons. They are usually facing a crisis moment, or they are at a crossroads.

WORDS OF ENCOURAGEMENT

I want to encourage you at the outset of this book.

First, You Are Not Alone in Your Questioning

As I talk with my Christian friends and acquaintances, They speak of their discontent and anxiety. They seem just as confused about their greater purpose in life as those who do not call themselves Christians. I suspect that the vast majority of people alive today are not even coming close to living God's promises, purposes, or plans for their lives. They do not even begin to understand, appreciate, or believe in their uniqueness. That perhaps is why they have so little confidence in themselves. Too few grasp the fact that they were born equipped to do great things.

Henry David Thoreau, philosopher and author of *Walden*, remarked, "The mass of men lead lives of quiet desperation." Despair and tragedy are closely linked. A person who is living out a *nightmare* is not living out *dreams*! The greatest tragedy of all is for a person to be managed by circumstances and live a half-dead life.

In our world today, much effort, energy, and concern are directed toward making a living. I have worked in at least ninety nations, and

I have seen more serenity in a Chinese peasant's face than I have seen in the faces of many top executives in this and other "advanced" nations.

Why is that so? I believe one reason is that the Chinese peasant doesn't know what he doesn't have and will never have. The executive is filled with anxiety over what she has, what she won't have, and what she has missed. She is consumed with making and maintaining a living.

God calls us rather to "make a life." He is not as concerned about our jobs as He is about our character, our relationships, and our witness of faith.

Much of your questioning may lie at this root: your inner conflict over what you perceive to be your external life and your internal life—making a living versus making a life. The good news is that the Lord does not desire that you ponder these questions about your existence without giving you answers. He desires that your questions be answered so that you find wholeness and purpose. Indeed, He is the truth of the answer you seek, the answer that is necessary if you are to live the life you were meant to live.

Second, I Believe Our Creator Desires for Us to Live a Purpose-Filled Life on This Earth, for our Benefit and the Benefit of Others

I don't believe a purpose-filled life exists only in heaven. Some people say about life's questions and mysteries, "We'll understand it all in the by-and-by, when we get to heaven." I certainly believe that our understanding will be illuminated in heaven and that some things will remain mysteries while we are on earth, but I don't believe our purpose in living is intended to be one of those mysteries!

I believe our Creator expects us to discover His plan for our personal lives and to live it out. God gave us minds capable of reasoning and spirits capable of discernment. Further, He gives the Holy Spirit to us as believers to help in the reasoning and the discerning processes. We must face squarely the challenge of finding God, finding ourselves, and then claiming God's promises and plan for us.

We are quick to say in Christian circles that God sees the beginning from the ending of every situation. He knows all. In theological terms, He is omniscient—all-knowing and all-wise. God's infinite capacity to know encompasses all of history (which is humanmade time) and eternity. Nothing is a surprise to God, and nothing is secret from Him.

Therefore, God knows our personal histories from start to finish, even as He knows the full breadth of all human history from start to finish. The Bible presents this concept by saying that God knew us "before the foundation of the world" (Eph. 1:4). In other words, He always had us in mind, precisely as we are and for the precise time in which we live.

Furthermore, God has made it very clear in His Word that He knows us intimately, far better than we know ourselves. Isaiah declared that it is the "LORD who made you / And formed you from the womb" (Isa. 44:2). Jesus said, "I am the good shepherd; and I know My sheep, and am known by My own" (John 10:14).

To think that God knows us and has always known us is an awesome concept. If the God who knows all about everything is the Creator of our lives, then surely He knew every circumstance we would ever encounter prior to His creation of us. Knowing all, He implanted into our lives the exact set of His traits and gifts that each of us would need to be His person on this earth and to be a participant in the development of His kingdom. He had both *why* and *how* answers for our lives at the moment He created us and breathed His life force into us.

We were not created at random or without meaning. God built into us a very specific meaning and purpose, and then He allowed us to be conceived and given birth to at a very specific time.

You and I are part of a master plan that boggles our imaginations. The more you contemplate the intricacies of God's design and the detail with which He has executed that design, the more awesome God becomes to you. He alone is worthy to be worshiped with your highest devotion and adoration!

GOD HAS A PLAN FOR YOUR SERVICE

The more we understand how God has shaped us and made us who we are, the more we are aware of God's individualized plan for our service.

More than a thousand references in the Old and New Testaments tell us that God has a plan for our lives. God has a master thought for each of His children. He is eager to share that thought with us. This thought is His destiny for us. It involves the service that He desires for us to render to others and to Him.

The master thought of God for you might be stated as God's mission, path, calling, direction, or leading. It points toward a divine goal.

Most Christians can recite readily the words of the Lord's Prayer, which includes this section: "Your kingdom come. / Your will be done / On earth as it is in heaven" (Matt. 6:10). I encourage you to pray, "Your will be done in me. I am part of Your earth, Your clay, for which You, the Master Potter, have a design." Having God's kingdom manifested in your life—God's purposes for you brought to fruition on the earth, even as they were designed and planned in heaven—is what the LifePlan process is all about.

In your giftedness and in your call to specific service, you will encounter *the life you were meant to live!*

2

AWAKENING TO YOUR GIFTEDNESS

Most people aren't living the life they were meant to live because they don't know who they are or what gifts God has given to them.

Living the life you were meant to live means living the life that God means for you to live, and that He has meant for you to live prior to your conception. Perhaps the most important concept for you to understand as you approach the LifePlanning process is this:

> *A LifePlan is God's plan for your life. It is not a plan that you conceive and develop, but a plan that you discover through a series of helpful exercises and processes.*

In our culture, we are so accustomed to the word *planning* being used by human beings and organizations that you may have assumed that the word *LifePlan* relates to a human planning process. It does not.

I have been involved in developing strategic plans for some of our nation's leading corporations for several decades. I understand very well the human planning process and the engineering of a comprehensive design that establishes goals, assigns component parts of those goals to specific individuals or work groups, and places the completion of those goals and subset goals on a schedule.

LifePlanning, however, is not a human-engineered, strategic-planning process. God established your LifePlan prior to your conception. You are the execution of *His* LifePlan—you are His creation and His instrument, placed into His timetable, specifically designed and shaped to bring Him glory.

In the LifePlanning process of discovery, you will have an opportunity to step back and see your life as a whole. Then you will gain a new perspective on how you have arrived where you are today and, therefore, what the next logical steps for your life may be.

A PROCESS OF DISCOVERY

So many of us are accustomed to making plans that the concept of discovering a plan is foreign to us. My contention, however, is that God has a plan for your life. He made you with certain traits and abilities—which I call your giftedness—so that you might fulfill a specific role and purpose. In creating *who* you are, God simultaneously built into your life *what* you are to do. When you discover His intent and fully embrace His plan, you are then able to live the life you were meant to live.

A current fad of feel-goodism in our society involves talking yourself into success. But what happens if you feel good about yourself and fail? What happens when a person has the most toys but still feels despair? What happens when you just can't talk yourself into the success you want to have?

The alternative approach is to recognize that God has a plan for each and every individual. God's definition of *success* is that a person find God's plan and live it out. Having the most toys and feeling good about yourself are ultimately irrelevant. Doing what God has created you to do is what will count, not only now but for all eternity.

Therefore, my supreme word of advice to you is this: *discover God's LifePlan and live it!*

YOUR BEING DETERMINES YOUR DOING

You begin by discovering who you are. Out of that understanding, you discern what you are to be doing.

For example, if you come to an understanding that you were created with the gifts of organization and combining working parts, you may very well conclude that God created you to be an engineer. If that indeed is the case, then doing the work of an engineer will bring you fulfillment and satisfaction. Or if you recognize that you were created to paint, you then must paint. Nothing else will be as exhilarating or as meaningful to you.

In contrast, if you were born with heavy bone structure, have always struggled with large-muscle coordination, and seem to have little sense of rhythm, you will be very frustrated in a pursuit of ballet, no matter how much you may think you have been created to be a ballet dancer. God didn't equip you to be a ballet dancer; therefore, you aren't likely to be a very good one, regardless of the effort you exert or the desire you say you have. At that point, it is time to think again, to discern more clearly.

You have been shaped a certain way—psychologically, intellectually, emotionally, physically, environmentally, historically, relationally, and above all spiritually—to fulfill a certain role, do certain work, and produce certain results. As you fulfill what you are to be and do, you experience personal satisfaction, peace, and joy. You have a certainty in your spirit that you are fulfilling God's plan and purpose for your life. When you are frustrated or anxious, or have a nagging feeling that you are out of sync, the likelihood is that you are operating outside God's plan. You need to reevaluate your life and gain a new perspective on who you are and what you are to be doing.

Flowers have no difficulty knowing God's LifePlan for them. They are to grow, bloom, provide nectar, and propagate. They have no self-will. They simply execute God's LifePlan for them. In like manner, animals have no difficulty knowing God's LifePlan. They grow, eat the things they are created to eat, produce the by-products they are supposed to produce, procreate, and do their instinctual best to stay alive as long as possible.

We human beings, however, seem to struggle mightily with the two profound philosophical questions that are born of our free will: Who am I? and Why am I here?

As I stated, the answers to these two questions are linked: who you are dictates, determines, or sets the direction for why you are here. Who you are is a composite set of God's gifts into your life. His gifts include not only your talents, traits, and innate abilities, but also the people He has placed in your life, the environment in which He has set you, and the experiences He has brought your way.

THERE WILL NEVER BE ANOTHER YOU

Talents are God's gift to each person. Talents are highly varied and very specific. The composite set of talents given to a person are that person's giftedness.

Your talents are your propensities, your "bent." They can take expression in many forms. The varied expression of a talent over a lifetime can add richness and depth to your life. It can also heighten your contribution.

You need to recognize several things about the talents God has given you.

You Are Unique!

You have been given a unique set of talents. God has breathed uniqueness into each person through the talents He has given. Each of us is as different as a snowflake, and we know that of the trillions of snowflakes, no two have ever been found to be identical. Each of us, with no exception, will be dispensed with. We will die, but none of us can be replaced.

You are unique.

You are created in God's image.

You are somebody.

God has made you in the image of His Son, Jesus Christ, and He desires that you grow into His likeness. He has a plan and a purpose for your life on earth, and also for your eternal life.

There has never been another you.

There will never be another you.

You are one of a kind in the history of the world.

God breaks the mold after each person is created.

I will praise You, for I am fearfully and wonderfully made;
Marvelous are Your works,
And that my soul knows very well. (Ps. 139:14)

The purpose for your life is to put your God-given gifts to work for good in your generation and in your sphere of influence. In putting your giftedness to work for God's purposes, and in moving from self-centeredness to Christ-centeredness, you will experience a radiant, totally *alive* life.

For whatever length of time God has planned for you to be on this earth, you are an irreplaceable person in God's eyes, and you are vital to the implementation of God's plan for this earth.

A LifePlan facilitator, Char Lindner, once said during my explanation of giftedness, "What you are really saying is that our giftedness is our spiritual DNA." She was exactly right!

Your Uniqueness Is Good

As a masterpiece of God's workmanship, you are a good creation. A master craftsman acquires or makes only the best tools. The same goes for God, our Master Craftsman. He creates no junk. Your talents are good, and you are to use them for good, bringing glory to the Source of all good.

A master craftsman makes a tool, produces a product, or executes a design with an exact purpose in mind. The tool and its purpose go together; one fits the other. God gave you talents so that you might use them perfectly in a very specific role. Jesus made this very clear in His parable of the talents. Those who used their talents saw them multiplied, and in the end, they were given even more talents and enlarged responsibility. The one who failed to use his talent had it stripped away. (See Matt. 25:14–29.)

God's plan will be for your personal good, resulting in a triumphant life of contribution, emotional fulfillment, and unending spiritual growth. It will promote life, not destroy it. It will result in your eternal and intimate relationship with your Creator. It will be for the good of others. It is a life that brings joy and abiding peace.

Your Uniqueness Is Tied to What You Can Do Well

Your potential for excellence lies within your uniqueness.

When I facilitate the discovery of a LifePlan for a person, I always give the person permission to explore fully what he or she can do well. The emphasis is never on what a person cannot do. I never address "weaknesses." You contribute through your gifts. This should be your focus. God doesn't give you weaknesses. In a real sense, they are a manmade, destructive myth.

Most people have been told all of their lives what they cannot do, should not do, or will not do. Very rarely do I encounter people who have been encouraged from birth to explore their unique talents and abilities and to pursue them to the highest and utmost of their energy.

I met a man who said that from his earliest memories, his mother had told him that God was calling him to be a doctor. When a parent gives a child such a message from birth, it is very difficult for that child to differentiate between the parent's voice and God's voice. The man naturally and automatically grew up believing that he was destined to become a physician. Years later—long after he had completed medical school and was a practicing physician—he admitted to me that he felt something was missing in his life. He felt maladjusted and anxious. He suspected that he had abilities that weren't being tapped, potential that wasn't being fulfilled.

How right he was! As he explored more and more of his God-given traits, he came to a startling conclusion: "God didn't create me to be a medical doctor." He didn't truly like his work. He didn't enjoy being around sick people, and he felt very little empathy for them. He liked to solve problems, but always struggled in his effort to limit his problem-solving efforts to a patient's physical ailments. He resented the long hours and arduous demands that he felt the medical profession required of him. He resented the hours spent away from his family and other pursuits that he truly found enjoyable. As I probed his feelings regarding the medical training he had undergone, I discovered that he hadn't really enjoyed science classes, even though he had earned high grades in them.

Mom, not God, had made a doctor.

Who had God made? The more this man explored his divinely crafted gifts and traits, he began to uncover his real passions and desires. He then had to make a serious decision: to continue in a line of work that he had pursued for fifteen years and from which he earned a great deal of money and received a certain amount of social status, or to do what truly fulfilled his God-given purpose on earth. He still is in the process of making that decision. As I always recommend, he is including his wife in the making of the decision. My guess is that he is very close to leaving the medical profession for a different line of work, and that when he does, he will find joy and exuberance for living that he has never known.

Ideally there comes a point when a person says about a situation or task, "This fits me." The way in which she is living and the things she is doing are completely comfortable to her and yet challenging at the same time. Not only does she sense a perfect fit, but she loves what she is doing and can't get enough of doing it. Furthermore, she is good at doing what she is gifted to do.

A synergy always exists among these factors: liking what you do, being gifted at what you do, and succeeding to the point of excellence at what you do.

People who are gifted in music generally do not need to be told that they are musically talented. They readily can tell that they have an ability to sing or play a musical instrument. Furthermore, you don't have to tell gifted musicians to enjoy music. They do so automatically.

You don't have to browbeat them to practice; they delight in practicing because they enjoy good music and want to be able to play musical pieces to the best of their ability. Gifted musicians never feel better or have a greater sense of purpose and fulfillment than when they are engaged in the performance of their gift.

This same combination of excellence, enjoyment, and giftedness exists for every type of talent or combination of talents.

YOUR GIFTEDNESS IS PRESENT FROM YOUR BEGINNING

Giftedness manifests itself in different ways at various seasons of life and in various domains of life. You may not always be called to fill a specific role or to function in specific ways. Your giftedness, however, remains. It is like a well from which water can be drawn and then applied to different purposes.

Once when my wife, Ginny, was just a little girl visiting her ailing grandmother, she mixed salt in a glass of water, and then said as she handed her grandmother the concoction, "I help you get well." The last thing that hypertensive grandmother needed was a glass of salt water, but out of her love for Ginny, she drank it. The fact is, Ginny had a heart for helping people from the time she was born. Her desire to see others get well was built into her by her Creator. It is absolutely no surprise to me that Ginny found fulfillment in her life in working as a nurse. God made her to be one! The traits emerged at a very young age.

You Must Discover Your Gifts

Your giftedness is *your* giftedness. It may be quite different from that of your siblings or your parents.

So many people I know suffer from low self-appreciation because they never heard words of approval, worth, or value from their parents. The fact is, many parents expect their children to live up to their standards or, even worse, to live the life the parents want the children to live. We all know of mothers who desire for their sons to be leaders and their daughters to be movie stars. I have met countless parents who were totally oblivious of the God-given talents and traits in their children, much less willing to admit that those talents and traits were different from their own.

> *My frame was not hidden from You,*
> *When I was made in secret,*
> *And skillfully wrought in the lowest*
> *parts of the earth.*
> *Your eyes saw my substance, being yet*
> *unformed.*
> *And in Your book they all were written,*
> *The days fashioned for me,*
> *When as yet there were none of them.*
> (Ps. 139:15–16)

No Elite Families

An interesting aspect of giftedness is that God in His infinite wisdom is not about to have any one family become the elite in His kingdom. We all can point to examples of this in the world at large. A president of the United States, Abraham Lincoln, came from frontier folk, parents who were poor and nearly illiterate. It has happened in the past, and it can happen again. Giftedness is not passed down from generation to generation as physical traits appear to be.

Some psychological traits seem to be passed down from fathers to sons or from mothers to daughters. Very often these "traits," however, are learned behaviors. An abused child becomes an abusive parent, for example. Abuse is not a part of a person's spiritual DNA. It is a learned behavior.

A person might say, "I received my quick temper from my father," or "I'm a compulsively neat person like my mother." In both cases, these are learned behavioral traits, not marks of God's giftedness.

You must be very clear on this point. God's gifts to you are always positive. They are traits and propensities within you for good.

God places these good traits into children without regard to the family's status, lineage, culture, or finances. Great artists and musicians are born into rich and poor families alike, in every culture around the world. Just because a person's father is gifted to be a painter or his mother is gifted to be a musician does not lead us to conclude that the person will be either a painter or a musician. He might be gifted to be an auto mechanic!

Too often we expect the children of achievers to be achievers in the same field—or at the very minimum, in a closely related field. That is rarely the case.

A Random Distribution of Gifts

In my opinion, God has distributed His gifts randomly.

In past years, I thought that in some mysterious ways, the genes in a family tree wore out—a burst of greatness used up the last of a family's genetic energy. The more I studied this, the more I realized that there is no such thing as genetic burnout. What we have, instead, is a choice by God that His giftedness will be assigned randomly throughout the human race to ensure two things: first, that all jobs get done, and second, that gifted individuals are always compelled by those around them to remain humble and to use their gifts for service.

> *God's gifts have been distributed at random.*

This second point is significant to the kingdom of God. If strains of people were all gifted in certain ways, it would be very easy for pride to take hold and to keep gifts from being shared or used for the good of all. God's gifts to us are always intended for use in service or ministry. Furthermore, the elite in the world rarely become true disciples—their pride keeps them from humbling themselves before God and submitting their will to that of the Holy Spirit.

This acknowledgment that God's gifts are given at random should be a comfort to many parents who question why their son or daughter isn't succeeding to the same degree that they have. The son or daughter may not have been gifted by God in the same way. It has absolutely nothing to do with what the parent has done or not done.

A parent's role is not to pass along gifts to children. Rather, a parent's responsibility is to protect and provide for children, to train them in the way of the Lord, and to help them discover and develop the gifts that God has placed in their lives. God is the giver of every good and perfect gift. He is the One who distributes His gifts as He wills.

I heard about a man who was a brilliant scientist. He couldn't understand how his son had no aptitude for math and science but enjoyed the study of literature. He felt that his son had in some way betrayed him. He even said, "He's not my son"—not that he disowned the boy, but that he felt no kinship with his son. What a sad conclusion! The father could have learned so much from his son and helped his son in many ways to appreciate his unique giftedness. Instead, the boy grew up feeling undervalued, unappreciated, and a failure in his father's eyes.

The very simple fact is this: the father had been gifted in the abilities useful in the study and application of science and math. The son had been gifted by God in an appreciation for literature.

No Gift Is Better Than Other Gifts

As you awaken to your giftedness, recognize that no gift is better than another gift. Physical strength is not universally better than mental strength, nor is mental strength universally the greater gift. Each gift is of equal value in and of itself. The *application* of a gift to a particular circumstance, need, or problem gives it value.

An associate pastor of a very large church came to me for the facilitation of a LifePlan. He had been given extensive pastoral duties but could not readily offer solace. Yet he was a detail person and very good at administration. In the course of our time together, I told him that I knew his senior pastor and that he needed an administrative pastor on his staff. "That should be you," I said. "Pastoral care is not the way you have been shaped by God."

At first, he was reluctant to agree with me. Why? Because he had always thought of pastoral counseling and the pastoral gifts as being the highest a clergyperson could possess. However, the more he saw his gifts, the quicker he was to agree. He later proposed to his senior pastor that he take on the detailed administrative responsibilities of the church. The pastor turned them over to him with relief. The associate pastor couldn't be happier in his new role. He is doing the job he was shaped by God to do.

GIFTEDNESS IS TIED TO A SPECIFIC ROLE

Each of us was created for a specific role in relationship to others.

Dwight David Eisenhower fully developed his incredible talents. He had administrative-leadership skills to organize, manage, and lead the Allied invasion of Europe in World War II. He later served as our president, employing those same talents in the governance of the nation.

General George Marshall was also a highly talented man. His talent, however, was in strategic-leadership ability—a talent he employed in developing the incredible plan for the Allied invasion. At the end of the war, as secretary of state, Marshall used his skill to conceive what became known as the Marshall Plan. Through it, Europe and Japan were reconstructed. We fed, we trained, we rebuilt—we treated vanquished people as no other nation in history ever had.

Each man wisely functioned in his element. Marshall was the man gifted to carry out the job of making the strategic plan. Eisenhower was the man gifted to carry out the job of executing the plan. Marshall used his gifting to develop a brilliant strategy; Eisenhower used his gifting to execute superbly. President Franklin Roosevelt had the wisdom to assign these leaders to the right jobs, jobs God had made the men for. The result was a successful conclusion to one of the most devastating wars in history.

All Jobs Get Done

Have you ever pondered the awesome mind of God who orchestrates talents so that all tasks—all things essential to life and progress—get done? Someone writes the music, engineers the buildings, keeps the books, nurses the ill, protects the neighborhood, cares for the forest, grows the food. All jobs get done.

God's gifts are distributed in such a way that all jobs get done.

Each of us is shaped or "wired" for a specific role. There is no job that *doesn't* get done, to some degree and in some fashion.

All of this is by design. I believe it is one of the surest proofs of God's existence and of God's nature as a Master Planner and a Master Designer. It is no accident that all jobs get done.

In addition, God has made provision for getting some jobs done during the day and some done at night because certain services are needed on a twenty-four-hour basis. He has gifted certain people to be day people and others to be night people.

God has provided each person with a set of gifts that, taken as a whole, allow humanity to function. Nothing that humankind as a whole needs in the way of services and talents has been omitted at any given time in history.

In an ideal world, every person would be doing precisely what he or she was created to do. That may be a good definition of heaven. We certainly can envision that if each person on earth were doing precisely what he or she was created to do, and doing it at the God-designated ideal time of day, there would be far less work-related stress in this world. Each person would find his or her job to be possible—with a high rate of success—as well as pleasurable and meaningful.

That doesn't mean that all stress would evaporate because much of life's stress and turmoil is related either to sin or to faulty relationships, not tasks. Nevertheless, a significant amount of stress would be eliminated if all people were doing on a daily basis what they were created to do.

Too many people think of themselves as I once did—as a nobody trying to become a somebody. God saw me as a somebody all along, just as He sees you as a somebody. Time and again I hear people describe themselves as "I'm just a . . ." Nobody is a "just a" anything. You are eternally valuable to God, and He has created you for a vital role in His amazing plan and purpose for the world.

THE KEY TO PERSONAL SATISFACTION

Fulfilling your unique role is the key to achieving personal satisfaction. When you are truly and fully living the life you were meant to live, you'll have an abiding sense of both purpose and delight.

God's mission will always fit you so that there is no emotional, psychological, or spiritual chafing. God is the Master Tailor, the One who has designed the role that is perfectly suited to the person He has created. That is the picture we have when Jesus said, "My yoke is easy and My burden is light" (Matt. 11:30).

A yoke that is perfectly crafted for a specific animal—one carved to fit with precision and comfort the neck of an ox or horse—is easy to carry. It is not a burden. It doesn't rub raw. Jesus was telling His disciples that the character traits, the mission, the life He meant for them to live would fit them perfectly. It would not be a burden to do what the Holy Spirit prompted them to do; it would be a joy and a delight.

Joy and Self-Affirmation

People who live out God's plan and purpose inevitably come to like, affirm—yes, even love—themselves.

Some Christians find the concept of self-affirmation or self-love to be troubling. For centuries, the historical and religious concepts of self-denial and guilt have been taught, and we have as our first response to pleasure or abundance, "No, I can't have that or be that. I shouldn't want that. I'm not worthy. I must not think too highly of myself."

In other words, we say to ourselves in the face of the things we call good and desirable, "I don't deserve it; I'm not good enough to expect it; I'm not worthy of receiving it." This thought process has caused many people, Christians included, to downplay their talents, underrate their potential for making a valuable contribution, or undermine their ability to release fully their God-given potential. Each of us is a master of self-criticism. We need no help at this.

While we know that life on earth will never be perfect because of sin, we also are told in God's Word that life is intended to be a grand experience for believers in Christ Jesus. I encourage you to embrace fully the concept that God has more for you to be, more for you to do, and more for you to enjoy. He loves you. He calls your giftedness good. He expects you to love yourself as His creation and to delight in the gifts He has given you.

Why am I so certain that life is meant to be a joyous growth experience? Because God made us with vast capacities both to grow and to experience joy. God's plan is that we be fully, radiantly alive. He is the Source of an exuberant, vibrant life. As Jesus said, He came to give us life "more abundantly" (John 10:10).

I believe that as you discover who you are, and how you might grow in your gifts and into a greater likeness of Jesus Christ, you will come into the greatest joy and fulfillment you can ever know.

One of the most dramatic examples of this that I have witnessed was in the life of a neighbor who admitted to me one day, "I run this roofing company because I married the daughter of the owner of this roofing company. That's the only reason. I hate my job."

I asked, "What would you really like to be doing?"

He said, "I'd like to be teaching high school history."

"Why don't you do that?"

"I'd lose too much."

I responded, "Consider what you would gain."

A couple of years later, that man had reached the point where he hated his job with such intensity that it was affecting his health and definitely impacting his marriage. He partially blamed his wife for his unhappiness and ill health since she wanted him to run her daddy's company and refused to acknowledge his unhappiness as being valid.

All in a day, that man resigned from the roofing company, filed divorce papers, and moved as far away as possible from his "old life." He went back to college to renew his teaching credentials and became a history teacher in a rural school system. He lived a simpler life in a more laid-back environment, and the last I heard, he had found great satisfaction in his life. He told more than one mutual friend that he hadn't known it was possible to feel such peace and joy on a daily, ongoing basis.

I certainly don't advocate divorce, and I believe that had he faced his hatred for running the roofing company earlier and with a different spirit, his marriage may very well have been saved. But I can applaud his decision to live according to the way God had created him, rather than to live according to the dictates of other people who had little interest in the graces of God manifested in his life.

Anytime someone acts primarily to fulfill the expectations of another person—rather than to fulfill the precise and unique purpose of God—that person is going to be miserable, unfulfilled, and less than whole. Anger, resentment, bitterness, and hate are very likely to manifest themselves—some of which may be expressed outwardly, but all of which will burrow deep within and destroy the person from the inside out.

Conversely, someone who follows God's LifePlan experiences deep personal fulfillment. Peace and joy are always evident.

God has given each of us a unique set of gifts. When we discover them, we delight in them. We enjoy using them. We appreciate others who are gifted in the same way. We find purpose in practicing our gifts and cultivating them.

More Like Play than Work

People who are moving within their gifts and developing their gifts rarely feel as if they are working. The effort seems more like recreation or play. The growth of a gift requires effort and diligence, but the effort and the learning are enjoyable. The diligence is desirable. They *want* to do what God has called them to do.

A designer was hired to build a full-scale model of a project. He was gifted to do that kind of work, and he had no difficulty at all in staying up until midnight painting figurines, planting "trees," and working on the details of the model. It was play to him!

The Lord's desire is that you truly *live the life you were meant to live*—experiencing not only peace of mind and peace of soul, but also an exhilaration that comes with a recognition that your life counts, that it is worthy and valuable to God and to others.

NOT A MATTER OF PREDESTINED ENGINEERING

Does all of this sound like error-proof, predestined engineering to you? Far from it.

In creating you, God gave you free will. He allows you to choose whether you will fulfill His LifePlan for you or attempt to make a plan of your own. Furthermore, He gives you freedom to choose the way you will express yourself as you fulfill His LifePlan. Hundreds of millions of details are left to your creative choices.

The development of your talents is a matter of your free will. You alone can choose to turn your God-given talents into genuine mastery. Undeveloped talents can be used only for lesser purposes. Developed talents can be used for higher and higher purposes, as God desires.

You are not a robot. You are a wonderfully fashioned human being, created by God, in the image of God, and for God's purposes—but also as a friend to God, a living creature apart from God, a person designed for fellowship with God. God delights in the way you choose to express yourself within the parameters of His plan and purpose.

Your talents are a sacred trust. Once you catch hold of this concept and truly internalize it and make it a part of your thinking about yourself, you will begin to have the passion of a zealot. You will begin to consecrate your life to the fulfillment of your life's work. You will begin to see that your work is sacred. Your concern will be only that what you do pleases God. That's the point at which human planning enters the picture, and it is also the point that lies just beyond the last page of this book. The purpose of this book is to help you realize God's LifePlan for you. What you do with that realization is always up to you.

This book will help you discern more clearly who you are and, therefore, what you are to be about in your life. The exact action plan that you create for the pursuit of God's LifePlan is your responsibility. Your action plan will be a product of your free will.

This book provides exercises to help you gain a perspective on your giftedness and develop a deeper awareness of the many facets of your life that God has given you to develop.

Personality Is Retained

Your gifts are at the essence of who you are. They are major contributors to your personality, but they are not the sum of it.

The personality taken as a whole may be likened to the person with whom you fall in love. You love who the person really is, not just the way the person appears physically, the specific traits the person has, or specific deeds the person does. The whole is always more than the sum of the parts.

When you surrender to Christ, you surrender self-will, but you retain your persona. This is unlike the demands of all false-religion cults, which demand that a person give up personality and become uniform to the group in thoughts, dress, actions, and words. God does not desire that you become uniform with others, all of the same ilk. He desires that you be in relationship with Him in the fullness of yourself, your will totally yielded to Him and your identity rooted and grounded in Christ Jesus, with your uniqueness retained. Fleshly desires are stripped away, but your one-of-a-kind personality remains.

The apostles Paul, Peter, and John had very different personalities. Paul was transformed from a zealous slayer of Christians to a zealot for Christ. Peter's stubborn nature was transformed into the strength of the rock upon which the church was built. John's loving nature was transformed into a passion for Christ so consuming that his gospel is unique in its presentation of the path to eternal life. They retained their individuality, unique callings, and means of expression. Yet each man was totally surrendered to Christ Jesus. In the spirit realm, they had great commonality because they operated under the direction of the same Holy Spirit. In the natural realm, although they were transformed from their worldly natures to have renewed minds in Christ, they functioned as separate and distinct individuals. In like manner, so do we.

TALENTS ARE MEANT TO BE EMPLOYED WITH LOVE

God's desire is that you wrap your talents in love as you use them to benefit others.

Mother Teresa wrote about this subject:

> We have all been created for greater things—to love and to be loved. Love is love—to love a person without any conditions, without any expectations. Works of love are works of peace and purity. Works of love are always a means of becoming closer to God, so the more we help each other, the more we really love God better by loving each other. Jesus very clearly said, "Love one another as I have loved you." Love in action is what gives us grace. We pray and, if we are able to love with a whole heart, then we will see the need. Those who are unwanted, unloved, and uncared for become just a throwaway of society—that's why we must really make everybody feel wanted.[1]

Lyrics to a wonderful song by Sir Andrew Lloyd Webber proclaim, "Love changes every thing."[2] For a surrendered Christian, these lyrics really do sum up the meaning of life. To really live is to be madly, totally in love with our Lord.

Recently I held my newborn great-grandson, Austin-Wayne, in my arms. As I looked at his perfect little body and felt his strong grip on my finger, I had a strong awareness that I was holding a part of God's future design. My great-grandson is a part of humankind's renewal, of God's provision for continuity. Great feelings of love for my grandson filled my heart. He may not know the depth of my love *now,* but I still offer that gift of love to him, knowing that it will act like a magnet between us as he grows older. There is nothing that I would desire to withhold from him as he grows in his ability to accept my gifts of love.

Love takes many forms, but in all cases, it fills us with a passion and faith to *give* to those we love. In our giving lies our true self-actualization. It is in giving that our potential is released.

Talents might exist, be recognized, be developed, and even be employed, yet still not bring an abiding sense of personal value and worthiness *if they are employed void of love.* Doing what you are good at doing brings some satisfaction. But doing what you are good at doing with the intent of expressing love to another person? That brings the ultimate feeling of self-fulfillment!

God's master key to happiness is giving ourselves away.

Part of the love factor in our lives is intended by God for inward application. We are to love ourselves. In receiving God's love and forgiveness, we are to forgive ourselves. We are to recognize that God's giftedness to us is an expression of His love; therefore, our gifts are expressions of our value as human beings. We must neither deny nor denigrate our gifts. We must not long for or be jealous of the gifts of others. God has created us in His way, out of His love. In loving God, we must accept His giftedness as His will, His choice and, ultimately, His expression of love to us. We cannot say we love God and then hate who He has made us to be!

In like manner, we cannot say we love God and then express hate for the way He has made others to be. The expression of love requires that we accept the unique giftedness of other individuals and encourage them to recognize, develop, and then use their talents for the good of others. We must not seek to manipulate other people or to require them to display gifts they do not have. We must see them as God sees them—uniquely gifted people with a specific role to fill in God's master design for all of humanity and all of eternity.

To love others is to bond with them, to join hands and heads and hearts and giftedness. Christ called His people to be His body. Each person is naturally gifted or endowed with specific talents intended for consumption or use by others. We are continually to be in both give and receive modes.

In a web structure, all fibers reinforce one another. A web is, in fact, God's strongest structure. A web structure is God's intended design for the family, for the body of Christ, for God's "team" of people on the earth. Each of us is to become a fully functioning member of a godly community with a role to fill that invariably involves other people. In return, we have needs that only the giftedness of others can fill in our lives.

A mutuality of appreciation for and a sharing of giftedness is God's design. When we truly grasp this truth, we will find ourselves much more willing to develop and use our gifts. In asking God to help us identify and develop our gifts, we also must ask Him to help us grow in our love for others so that our gifts might be rightly and fully used.

> *When we give others the gift of ourselves—our time, our talent, our love, our presence—we give them the most precious gift we can ever give. The same is true for our giving of self to God.*

SOME TALENTS ARE SOLELY FOR BEAUTY

You are not only a functional creation, of course. The Master Craftsman is also the Supreme Artist. He has created you to execute your function and fulfill His LifePlan with a flair and style all your own. Nobody will do what you do, and nobody could possibly do it like you will do it—indeed, as only you can do it.

Beauty abounds everywhere—in people, in creatures, in breathtaking vistas. We live under a beautiful vaulted dome, called sky, which on clear nights bathes the earth and seas with the glow of galaxies. All around us we see the incredible natural beauty of the world—the majesty of lands and seas, the riot of color in a meadow of wildflowers, the endless diversity in plant and animal life. When I drive through Maui's rain forest on the road to Hana, I always stop to admire the rainbow tree, a gum tree that glows with every color of the rainbow.

Why was the rainbow tree created? Why did God make the wildflowers? Was it a functional necessity for my life? No. God delights in giving us endless forms of beauty simply so that we might enjoy them. Granted, they are a part of God's functional design for all creation, but as these creations impact us individually, they are not for our use as much as for our pleasure. It's as if God speaks to us, "Take delight in My work. Be inspired. Be filled with a sense of wonder and awe. See My hand everywhere." Beauty's purpose is to give us joy.

When you discover and use your gifts for the good of those you love and have chosen to serve, your life takes on beauty. It inspires others. It points toward the Creator. It brings glory to God.

Perhaps when all has been said, the highest purpose for your giftedness is just that: to portray the beauty of His holiness. If so, what a compelling reason to awaken to your gifts, to value and appreciate them, and to develop them!

3

GAINING A NEW PERSPECTIVE

No person can make a good estimate of distant lands from the floor of a valley. A person must get to a vantage point, a viewpoint from which one can see the full breadth of the valley and gain a view of the valleys that lie beyond it.

Ginny and I live in a mountain community high above the greater Los Angeles basin. We make frequent trips up and down the mountain in the course of business and pleasure trips.

One thing I have learned from living on a mountaintop is that we gain valuable perspective from a mountaintop vantage point. On a clear day as we descend the mountain, we can see for miles and miles across the valleys below us, out to the ranges of mountains lying to the south.

When I invite someone to come up to my mountain home office for a LifePlan consultation, I do so with a desire and an awareness that the person needs to gain a mountaintop perspective on his or her life. Everyone needs that perspective at least once in a lifetime and very probably a number of times.

Of course, you don't have to physically travel to a mountaintop to gain a big-view perspective. You can achieve such a perspective anytime you are willing to step back and take a diligent, thoughtful, and spiritually sensitive look at the full scope of your past, present, and future.

DISCOVERY OF AN EMERGING TRUTH

Much of the time I spend facilitating a LifePlan is devoted to helping a person gain perspective and discover an emerging truth about his or her life.

While truth is our goal and truthfulness the framework for gaining perspective, I also realize that many people do not readily know the truth of their own lives. It is not that they desire to deceive themselves but that they have never intentionally, and with concentrated focus, faced their lives. They have tended to see their lives in pieces, living in the present tense of what is happening to them and around them. The LifePlanning process allows them an opportunity to view the whole of life with the intent of discovering what God has done to bring them to the point where they are now.

Gaining perspective, then, is a process of emerging truth. Every aspect of the process is designed to provide another angle at understanding the whole. No single exercise or module allows us to understand truth fully, but each builds upon the other so that the truth emerges.

All people tend to hide the truth from themselves in order to feel better about themselves. Yet when you lay yourself open to the searching, purifying truth of God's Spirit, you are enveloped in the most gentle, loving, and forgiving revelation possible. The tears that may flow are ones not of anguish and despair, but of healing.

Many years ago a woman who had been abused by her father as a child came to me for a LifePlan facilitation. She was an outstanding aeronautical engineer. For decades she had lived in shame about her past, and her shame had led her to cut off a large portion of her life and to live in denial of it. To a great extent, she hated her life.

As she began to open herself to the full truth of who she had been created to be, and she saw how God had prepared and equipped her to survive her past, she experienced God's love and healing as never before. God had not caused her pain or shame. Rather, He had been present with her in her pain and continually had been shaping and molding her life and personality for His greater purposes and good. The tears that flowed brought release, relief, and a full surrender to the love of God. She faced the full truth of her life and found that because it was God's truth, it was and is good.

On another occasion, I worked with a top executive on a Life-Plan. We spent five full days together, and I recognized early in our sessions that he lived in tremendous fear of blowing it. He was an able and well-established executive, but he was not as loved in his company as he was at home. As we talked, he revealed that at his core was a deep fear that he could not or would not be able to do enough to win the approval and love he desired from his colleagues and employees.

Facing God's truth about our lives always results in something good.

As he looked back at his life, he faced the truth that his father had never expressed approval or love to him. Nothing that he did was quite good enough. He grew up with unrelenting criticism. My guess is that Dad was role-modeling the treatment he had received as a child; a dysfunctional cycle was repeating itself. All of his life, the man had worked hard to gain the approval of his father. This went on long after his father's death.

How did this manifest itself in the present moments of his work life? He turned a critical eye on his subordinates and peers. He was the same hard taskmaster to others as his father had been to him. At home, he was loving and kind because that was his turf—he felt no condemnation or criticism there. At work, he was at war, constantly seeking to prove himself.

When he faced the truth about his past and present, he wept openly for several minutes. His were tears of sorrow, genuine repentance and, ultimately, healing. He knew immediately what he needed to do in the future and the changes he needed to make in his life. He knew with a sure knowing what God desired for him to do and to be.

> *God has given us the ability to sense and find the truth before it finds us. When the truth finds us first, the results can be most unpleasant. Most of the time the signals are there to be discerned.*

Gaining perspective is, in many ways, a form of diagnosis. Medical research has concluded that 75 percent of a cure lies in an accurate diagnosis. The great physicians are those who are good diagnosticians. Without an accurate diagnosis, treatment can never be fully effective. The same is true in the discovery of your LifePlan. Unless you gain a full perspective on your life, you can miss your purpose for being.

A GENTLE PROBING

As you probe your life in the coming pages, be gentle but insistent with yourself. Don't back away from areas that seem painful. They are the very areas you probably need to face the most.

Don't condemn yourself as you probe. The discovery of your LifePlan is not intended to be an exercise in self-condemnation; it is an exercise in self-recognition and God-recognition. It is a staggering thought that God loves you and me as much as He loved His Son, Jesus. That is why He sacrificed Him for us. God loves each of us unconditionally, totally. The LifePlanning process is intended to help you gain a greater perspective on the whole of your life. If you leave out a particular aspect of your life, denying its impact or relevance, you will omit an aspect that is important to the whole.

TRUTHFULNESS IS PARAMOUNT

Gaining perspective is a process that unveils the truth of your life. The process is only as valid, however, as your willingness to face your life truthfully.

Paul wrote that "whatever things are true . . . meditate on these things" (Phil. 4:8). It was no accident that Paul began this passage in Philippians about our thought life and attitude with truth. First and foremost, we must be about the discovery of what is true in our lives. We must also recognize that a level of emotional maturity is necessary to be able to face, accept, and then use truth.

Throughout the years of my consulting career as a corporate strategic planner, I have spent literally thousands of hours in various companies with fairly small groups of top executives. In each setting, the goal has been to seek the truth about what the company is, what the company is doing, and where the company is going. If a company's executives are unwilling to face the truth about the company's past and present, there is no validity to the plans that they make.

> *Every plan I have ever done has been based on the biblical principle that the truth is the only solid foundation for a plan. Proverbs 12:19 speaks of the certainty of words of truth.*

The same is true for the individual. Unless a person is truly willing to face both past and present, any plans aimed at the future will be hollow and without firm foundation.

About the only time that I ever lose my cool with people is when I realize that they have lied to me or tried to deceive me. Truth must be valued—and especially so when one faces one's life. Peter Drucker has observed that it is foolish to fool others and criminal to fool yourself.

Your Responsibility to Truth

A LifePlan process is for those who are proactive toward their lives. The process results in wise counsel, but it is not a process intended for emotional or psychological counseling. It is not therapy intended to remedy, cure, or remediate problems in your life. If you need treatment for a dysfunction, seek out a therapist trained in that area. The LifePlan process should come later for you. LifePlanning is a process that requires maturity of emotions.

The LifePlanning process is for those who want more understanding, and it is for those who desire to reach what they believe to be a higher potential and to make a greater contribution with their lives.

The process calls for you to move beyond blame and excuses. Ultimately, you are the only one responsible for your happiness or the way you live your life.

From time to time men have come to me saying, "If only my wife would change. . . ."

I never allow that train of thought to continue. I quickly say, "We are here to gain a perspective on *your* life, not on your wife's life. When she feels a need to change, we may do a LifePlan for her. Your response to your life, including your response to your wife, is not bound to what your wife does or does not do. It is within your power and ability to gain a new perspective on your life regardless of what any other person does."

For some, I feel certain, the person who might be blamed subconsciously, if not consciously, is a parent, a supervisor or employer, a rebellious child, or a strict authority figure. If you are truly going to grow as a person, you must stop blaming anyone else for how you respond to life and for what you choose to do with your life. The only human being who has the authority to limit you or put boundaries on you is *you*. In a free society we are our own jailers, and some of us lock ourselves up and throw away the key.

The greater question to ask if you have a troublesome marriage, family life, or work relationship is, What can *I* do to change the way I currently respond?

Courage to Embrace the Truth

Change and discovery are threatening to many people. I encourage you to approach the LifePlan process with courage and boldness. Delight in what you discover. God has a desire for you to know what He will reveal to you in this process. He intends for this new awareness into your giftedness to be a blessing to you. His purposes are for good in your life.

> *Do not be deceived, my beloved brethren. Every good gift and every perfect gift is from above, and comes down from the Father of lights, with whom there is no variation or shadow of turning. Of His own will He brought us forth by the word of truth, that we might be a kind of firstfruits of His creatures.* (James 1:16–18)

NEW WAYS OF PROCESSING

In the search for perspective—in discovery of an emerging truth—the LifePlan process calls for you to deal with facts in these two ways:

1. Breakthrough thinking
2. Spiritual discernment

Each is important if you are to discover the *whole* truth about yourself. Breakthrough thinking is largely a rational, mental process. Spiritual discernment is largely an emotional, spiritual process. Both are required for understanding and for life to take on meaning.

BREAKTHROUGH THINKING

Breakthroughs in thinking occur when you carry thinking to the highest conceptual level. This is true mountaintop thinking. As I stated earlier about gaining perspective, you find it difficult to see far into the distance from the floor of a valley. From the mountaintop, however, you can see not only the valley and the mountain, but also the distant horizon. The same is true in thinking and planning.

> *"Come now, and let us reason together," says the LORD.* (Isa. 1:18)

As a believer, you need to recognize and actively claim with faith the fact that the Holy Spirit desires to help you think at the highest levels. The Holy Spirit has been made available to help you achieve breakthroughs in understanding. The Holy Spirit is certainly capable of entering the reasoning process and desires to do so. Your desire should be that the *Lord's* desire for your life is at the top of your mind, continually viewed in living color and in three dimensions.

The Use of a Matrix

A matrix connects information that helps you think at higher levels. A matrix is an intersection of data:

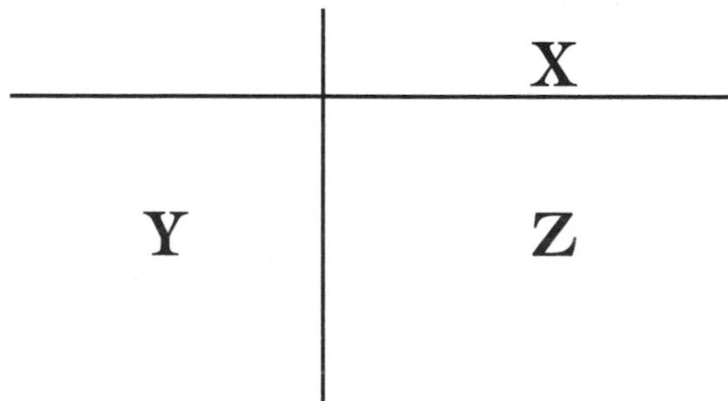

For example, you might have these two pieces of information:
X = I am 40 years old.
Y = My career is just plain work, one new job after the other.

The intersection of these two bits of data is going to yield a new level of meaning:

Z = I am having a career of "starts" in which I have no passion. I have never taken charge. It's about time I did!

The brain was designed for this type of intersecting process. The Nobel Prize–winner Gerald Edelman, one of the most knowledgeable brain researchers of our century, stated that the brain is capable of processing bits of data to at least 10^{800}. We do not even use 1 percent of this capacity. God has built into you the capacity to know yourself and to see the patterns of your life.

In various exercises in this book, you will be asked to seek out relationships, patterns, trends, and themes using a matrix. Ask the Holy Spirit to help you see the real purpose and meaning embedded in the data of your life as you connect bits of information to overall trends.

The Use of Charts

A method that I have found beneficial for many people is to make diagrams and charts. Charts put into visual form what people may only have thought, intuited or, in some cases, discussed verbally. We human beings, for the most part, learn through visual means. Some researchers have estimated that the average person learns more than 70 percent of all she knows through visual stimuli.

I have found value in charting visually what I hear my clients say to me. Many people have never seen the whole of their lives in a visual representation. The charts that I generate in a LifePlan facilitation are oversized pages that I mount on the walls of my home office. As we complete module after module, chart after chart, the graphic representation eventually covers three office walls and thus fills a person's peripheral view. All around him, the person sees his giftedness represented in words and charts.

Much of what happens after the walls are filled with these pages happens in silence. The person who has come for a LifePlan confronts his own life. Sometimes after seconds, usually after several minutes, an inner voice begins to speak to him—a revelation is birthed.

I encourage you to copy the various exercises in this book onto larger sheets and then post them as a composite in a space that is entirely your own and over which you have control. One man took home his LifePlan pages and posted them on the walls of his study. When he wants to review his life, he looks around the room. He has converted his study to be his Life Center!

Breakthrough Thinking in All Areas of Life

I find that breakthrough thinking occurs most often as people deal with vocations or careers. So many people perform jobs. They transfer from job to job. In many ways, their giftedness is wasted on jobs.

Breakthrough thinking results in our seeing that Christ has careers and roles in mind, not isolated jobs. He is molding us to *be* His people, not simply to do tasks. Life is not about making a living, but about *living*. For Christians, a career is not about money, but about fulfilling our calling. It is about seeing our work as ministry and about using our giftedness to bring glory to God on the earth.

Breakthrough thinking can and should be directed to every area of life. A number of people have come to a breakthrough point with regard to their marriages and families.

Too many people are locked into low-level thinking about their families: they seek to have a spouse and to have children. In high-level thinking, you come to see a spouse and children as God sees them—as the first and foremost field of ministry. The home is the crucible for the forging and living out of your faith. What does it mean to have a spouse or to have children unless you walk with those you love through the portals of heaven? While on earth, your family is a mission outpost of heaven, ordained to influence your neighborhood and community in positive ways.

As you work to gain a new perspective on your life, you will not have the advantage of a facilitator to help you—yes, even prod you—to higher-level breakthrough thinking. You must force yourself toward this. Continually ask yourself as you do the various modules in this book:

- What's the bigger picture here?
- How might God see this?
- What would Jesus desire to be done?

When you have a genuine breakthrough, you also experience a breaking away from the imprisonment of old patterns. Certain things from the past will no longer seem important or desirable. There is a sloughing away of the trivial. The old way of living is outmoded.

Breakthrough thinking is an important prerequisite to change. Require it of yourself.

SPIRITUAL DISCERNMENT

Breakthrough thinking is a process of reason. Spiritual discernment is a process involving the emotions and spirit. It yields spiritual meaning.

The same God who said to Isaiah, "Come now, and let us reason together," is the God who said through Christ, "Love one another." (See Isa. 1:18; John 15:17.) The mind and heart, or the intellect and the spirit, are intended to be in harmony and work together.

> ***You cannot come to full truth without spiritual discernment.***

If you are so emotional that you give no place to reason, you are not capable of making sound decisions. If you are stifled in your emotions and make all of your decisions solely on the basis of calculated reason, your decisions will be without passion or drive. The two are intended to be in balance.

You cannot come to full truth without spiritual discernment. Therefore, the LifePlan process requires that you be capable of spiritual processing. Such processing is available only to the Christian believer, in my opinion, for reasons I will outline here.

LifePlanning Is a Believer's Process

The LifePlanning process is for believers—those who have accepted the reality that God has made forgiveness of sin available through

His Son, Jesus Christ. In my experience, only the Christian truly desires that God's will be done, as opposed to self-will. The person who is seeking God, but hasn't accepted Christ, is still concerned primarily with self and what self can achieve. The person who has recognized that self is limited and fallible is most likely to desire to know God's plan.

The LifePlanning process also calls upon a person to ask for assistance from the Holy Spirit to aid in the discernment of one's own creation. The nonbeliever does not have access to the Holy Spirit's indwelling ability to aid in discernment.

LifePlanning, in my belief, is a holy process. Its aim is a balanced, holy, fully surrendered life. Its goal is to help you serve God in every domain of life, with Christ as your role model. It is living out God's plan and giving God the glory in everything you do. All of Him. Christ in all.

I once heard a pastor say, "Until we come to know our Lord, we cannot fully understand ourselves or truly believe in our potential." I believe he's right.

Discernment Is an Acute Spiritual Insight

For many people, discernment is something of a "stepping into the light" experience. One person described her LifePlan experience this way: "It was like walking through a previously closed door. I had always wondered what was on the other side—the hidden side of me. Now I know."

The key to recognizing life patterns, trends, and themes is discernment. Discernment is acuteness in judgment and understanding. It might be considered crystal-clear understanding. When you discern, emerging reality is so clear that it becomes present reality. Similarly, an unseen reality of the past, when discerned, becomes present reality. And it is reality—truth—past, present, and future, that provides the perspective through which a Life-Plan is formed.

Discernment results in new information, and new information inevitably compels a certain degree of change. Even if the LifePlan process only confirms what you have long felt to be true about your life, that confirmation can lead to more resolve, diligence, or focus.

Spiritual discernment is not an intellectual process. It is insight gained through a God-given inner sense of what is truth.

The English word *discern* comes from the Latin *discernere,* which means "to separate by sifting." God's plan very often unfolds for you as you sift through the various factors that make up your personality, your giftedness, and your personal history, all the while inviting God's Holy Spirit to reveal truth to you.

Do not be unwise, but understand what the will of the Lord is.
(Eph. 5:17)

These things are required for keen spiritual discernment:

- Belief in Jesus Christ; faith is the spiritual "sifter"
- An understanding of God's Word
- Reliance on the Holy Spirit for daily direction, decision making, and problem solving

Knowing Christ Is the Key to All

Many people have asked me, "Tom, how can I know God's will for my life?"

My first answer to them is the most important answer I can give, "Know Christ."

Those who ask me this question are generally looking for career guidance. My answer is aimed at pointing them toward the Supreme Career Guidance Counselor.

God's highest will for each of us is not that we choose to become a plumber instead of a lawyer, or a teacher instead of an insurance salesperson. God's highest will is that we know His living Word, His only Son, Jesus Christ, the very Word of God incarnate.

When I say this to people, they sometimes respond as if to say, "Well, yes, of course, but after that, how can I tell if I am to be a physician or a bond broker?"

Again, my answer is, "Know Christ."

I can't tell you whether you should be a pastor or a farmer. Christ can. He will reveal to you, on a daily basis and in a very personalized way, precisely what He desires for you to be and do in any given season of your life and in any circumstance in which you find yourself. No formula or career guidance matrix can do that for you, once and for all time.

Knowing that God's will for you is that you surrender your life fully to Christ Jesus and that you become completely submissive to the guidance and counsel of the Holy Spirit in your life is not ancillary advice for fulfilling your purpose in life. It is the ultimate advice. It is *the only advice* that counts eternally.

To know Christ is the only advice that counts for all of eternity.

This advice to "know Christ" is taken lightly by many Christian people, and is largely ignored as being impractical, because few people truly *want* to know Christ. They don't want to invest the time required to have a genuine intimate relationship with Christ, they don't want to learn how to have such a relationship, and they don't want to surrender their self-will, self-pride, self-centeredness, and self-determination. The Sunday morning creedal Christian will not know the fullness of life in Christ Jesus. If you are where I was—accepting of Jesus but not truly knowing Him—you have the most exciting adventure in living ahead of you.

To know Christ is the most practical advice I can ever give a person who is seeking direction in life. If you know the Son of God, and have through Him access to God's omniscience, omnipotence, and eternal unconditional love, then you are plugged into all that you will ever need in order to discover what you are meant to be and do—not only in broad generalized terms, but in very specific detailed terms.

If I were to tell you that I know a way for you to be 100 percent confident that you are being who you were created to be and doing what you were created to do every second of every minute of the remainder of your life, you would wait eagerly to hear that advice and likely be willing to pay a hefty fee to hear it. The fact is, I *do* know a way for you to be 100 percent confident that you are expressing and doing God's will every second of every minute of your life.

Know Christ. Surrender to Him. Learn to listen to His voice and then do what He says. Your deepest needs as you pass through life can be met only by Christ, your Source.

I have absolutely no doubt that the life God means for you to live is a life in which Christ becomes central to all of your decisions, thoughts, feelings, and actions. A life fully surrendered to God's purposes, and to living as Jesus lived in relationship to His heavenly Father, *is* the life God means for each person to live.

Not the same as knowing about Christ. Knowing Christ, as compared to knowing about Christ, is very much like the difference between falling in love with a person and knowing about a person.

Falling in love isn't the process of learning the biographical facts of a person's life or of reading a person's work résumé. Falling in love is relational. It is self-abandonment, a willingness to offer all of oneself to another person. If the beloved is also in love, she offers in return all that she is. As each person in a loving relationship gives all of himself or herself to the other person, a bond is forged, an intimacy grows, a knowing is experienced. There is a melding together of purposes, a uniting of hearts, a merging of life goals. The person who is in love longs to spend time with his beloved. He delights in doing what his beloved delights to do.

When you offer your all to God, who in response always offers His all to you, you likewise enter into a loving relationship. Your heart becomes one with God. You know God's thoughts, His desires, His purposes and plans, His will. You experience a growing communion with Him. You do not want to do anything that God has not directed you to do *with Him*. Your life is no longer singular. You are one with God; He is one with you.

Jesus is your strongest ally in your search for who you are and the life you were meant to live. In becoming human, Jesus took on all of the anxieties and sufferings of humanity. He has been through the struggles you go through. He has experienced what you experience in thoughts, emotions, and desires—albeit without sinning. If anyone is able to help you discover who you are as God's creation and what you were destined to do, it is Jesus—who knew fully who He was and what He was destined to do.

Christ is the fullness of life, the ultimate expression of a LifePlan that was perfectly executed. He is your role model of a LifePlan fully lived. You cannot know the full truth of your life unless you know Christ.

F. B. Meyer has written,

> Do not be afraid to trust God utterly. As you go down the long corridor you may find that He has preceded you, and locked many doors which you would fain have entered; but be sure that beyond these there is one which He has left unlocked. Open it and enter, and you will find yourself face to face with a bend of the river of opportunity, broader and deeper than anything you had dared to imagine in your sunniest dreams. Launch forth on it; it conducts to the open sea.[1]

I would add to that, "Do not be afraid to trust Christ. He will open to you the fullness of your life, now and into eternity."

HIS PLAN REVEALED IN HIS WORD

For a person to know a plan, it must be couched in language the person understands. I have done consulting in the Orient, but I can speak and understand only a few phrases in each of several Oriental languages. I can conduct a plan for the Japanese or Chinese, but I cannot present it *in* Japanese or Chinese. Our communication must be done in English.

God's plan for us to a great extent has been revealed in the written language of the Bible. Some people protest, "I just can't understand the Bible."

I believe the bigger problem is this: we can understand *enough* of the Bible to cause us to change our lives radically. However, I suspect that most of us want to do what we know the Bible says to do, but later, not now. We know the Bible is right, but we procrastinate. We blame our failure of behavior on a failure of understanding when our failure of behavior is a rebellion against our understanding.

A young boy overheard his mother and father discuss whether they were going to go to church on Sunday, given that their regular pastor was on vacation. The boy asked, "Are you thinking about not going to church on Sunday?"

His mother said, "Yes. A supply pastor is preaching, and supply preachers aren't always the best."

The boy replied, "Mom, the Word is the Word."

Wisdom from a young boy! The mother immediately replied, "You're right. We're going."

The Bible is our consistent fountain of wisdom. God also gives experiences and direct revelation, but to all people at all times in all situations, He has given His Word.

God will never call you to live a life that is in contradiction to His Word. He will never give you gifts, enable you to perform a task, or lead you in a direction that is in opposition to the Bible.

God's will is that you learn His Word, receive His Word, hear His Word, see His Word in action all around you, and then *do* His Word.

Accurate spiritual discernment must always be based on the foundation of the Word. Indeed, much of the life God desires for you to lead is clearly spelled out in the Scriptures.

The Old Testament presents a very clear picture of who God is as Creator and what God requires of us. We have a distinct message about where sin leads and where living in accordance with God's laws leads. The final words of the Old Testament are these:

> **And he will turn**
> **The hearts of the fathers to the children,**
> **And the hearts of the children to their fathers,**
> **Lest I come and strike the earth with a curse.**
> (Mal. 4:6)

In this one verse, we have a summation of God's desire, God's justice, and God's provision.

The New Testament presents a vivid picture of how God intends for us to live a life pleasing to Him. He shows us through His Son, Jesus Christ, both how to live that life and the provision He has made for us to receive forgiveness and enter into righteousness. The final words of the New Testament speak of God's ongoing provision for us through Christ: "The grace of our Lord Jesus Christ be with you all. Amen" (Rev. 22:21).

Jesus said of the Holy Spirit, "He will guide you into all truth; for He will not speak on His own authority, but whatever He hears He will speak; and He will tell you things to come. He will glorify Me, for He will take of what is Mine and declare it to you" (John 16:13–14).

God has made a very complete provision through His Word—His written Word; His incarnate Word, Jesus Christ; and His ever-present Word in us, the Holy Spirit—for us to know how God wants us to live. God has given a thorough revelation of Himself to us so that we might know about Him, and He has indwelt us with His very presence so that we might know Him personally in the depths of our spirits. There is nothing that we need to know about God or His overriding desire for us that has been hidden from us. His Word is there for the reading, there for the experiencing.

When we take God's Word into our lives as a whole, it gives us buoyancy. It brings us up in our spirits to the point that we can float above our circumstances, needs, and problems.

A Radically Different Life

The life God means for you to live as a Christian is radically different from that of the world at large.

The world sells the self-centered life. The prevailing message of the world is a one-word loop: *me, me, me*. To that end, you are encouraged to do, do, do, and buy, buy, buy. Success as the world defines it requires intense, self-focused personal effort, and this effort requires discipline, commitment, and self-focused goals. The end result is striving, striving, striving, and a very imbalanced life. Vocational life overwhelms all other life dimensions. There is minimal family life and probably no personal life. I know because I lived like this. That is *not* the life God intends for you—or me—to live.

The life presented in the New Testament stands in sharp contrast to what you see and hear advocated by today's self-help specialists. Read what Paul wrote to the early church at Philippi:

> **Be anxious for nothing, but *in everything by prayer and supplication, with thanksgiving, let your requests be made known to God;* and the *peace of God,* which surpasses all understanding, will guard your hearts and minds *through Christ Jesus.* Finally, brethren, whatever things are *true,* whatever things are *noble,* whatever things are *just,* whatever things are *pure,* whatever things are *lovely,* whatever things are of *good report,* if there is any virtue and if there is anything praiseworthy—*meditate on these things.* The things which you learned and received and heard and saw in me, these *do,* and the God of peace will be with you.** (Phil. 4:6–9, italics added)

Paul emphasized a quality of *being* that flows from having a relationship with Christ Jesus. If you were to ask me to describe in a nutshell the life that every Christian is meant to live, I would point you to this passage in Philippians. Let's take a closer look at the hallmarks of living described in this passage.

Peace of soul. The life you were meant to live is a life with peace of soul through Jesus Christ. It is a life that rests—with the deepest inner peace imaginable—in a complete union with Him.

Constant communication and trust. Living the life you were meant to live means being in constant communication with the Lord, trusting Him to help you manifest His life in every domain. It is living a life that is an unending prayer. It is a "heavenly" life lived out on this earth. It is not an easy life, but it is a possible life based on the following virtues:

- *True.* The world declares that a little deception is a clever tool to employ. The airwaves are filled with advertisements that entice you to deceive and that to a great extent are deceptions in themselves. Telling little white lies is considered acceptable by virtually everybody, especially if you can justify to yourself that it is the kind thing to do. A life of absolute truth requires vulnerability and accountability, and most people don't want the painful scrutiny that both involve.

- *Noble.* The world ridicules those who do the noble, honorable thing if it means personal loss. It may praise those who engage in noble acts of service if the acts are fleeting, but a life devoted to noble acts of service is classified by the world as unrealistic, out of touch with reality, or a life that should be cloistered. A person who is willing to turn the other cheek and give not only his coat, but also his cloak, is a chump, according to the world. A life of nobility requires a willingness to sacrifice the praise of people and to suffer personal loss.

• *Just.* The world tells us that justice is relative, and that although life should be fair, it never is. The world tells us that God's absolutes as expressed in the Bible are merely the suggestions of one type of religion about how to live a moral, ethical life, and that the suggestions of other types of religions are equally valid. A life rooted in God's justice requires a commitment to living in accordance with God's commandments and statutes, and an acceptance of God's plan for salvation. As one person said to me recently, "God is just, but thank God, He is also merciful." God's laws change not. God's provision for forgiveness is His greatest act of mercy to us.

• *Pure.* Our world is steeped in corruption, even as our earth is becoming saturated with pollution. We see corruption in every aspect of our culture. It is part of every organization; indeed, it is an indelible stain on every system of the world. To live a pure life is to say no to evil at every turn, to deny every temptation to sin. It is to be watchful at all times against the polluting spiritual influences of Satan. It is to choose to promote purity in an unclean world.

• *Lovely.* Our world lifts up the repellent. We are bombarded daily with messages that are shocking and that are intended to shock. The more gruesome the crime, the more awful the tragedy, the more horrible the consequences, the more piqued the curiosity of the masses. Living a life that is lovely requires turning away from much of the world's entertainment programming. It requires recognition and pursuit of God's perfection—in essence, learning to do things the way God does them, to design things the way God designs, to express yourself the way God expresses Himself.

• *Good report.* Newspapers and news programs emphasize the negative; it is their nature to do so. Tabloid journalism and tabloid broadcasting highlight aberrant behavior, not normative behavior. The world admires those who rebel, who seem to get away with a defiance of God's laws, and who live life on their own terms. In fact, our world is so eager to discover the bad in people that we seem to have lost all sense of the boundaries of privacy, decency, or propriety. To live a life that is of "good report," you must be willing to live in obscurity or face persecution aimed at defaming your reputation.

Opposition to the enemy. The Christ-centered life is in direct opposition to the enemy of your soul. Satan's devices are aimed at you on a daily basis to tempt you to pursue your life plan rather than God's LifePlan. You are bombarded and inundated with corrupting influences. Paul wrote, "Lest Satan should take advantage of us . . . we are not ignorant of his devices" (2 Cor. 2:11). The Christ-centered life is, in other words, no walk in the park. It is a life that is continually on guard against the many manifestations of evil.

The Ideal Can Be Real

You may be saying, "But this is the *ideal* life." Exactly. But because it is ideal does not mean that it cannot also be real. God intends for His people to have this type of life. Jesus sent the Holy Spirit so that we can live this life. We first, however, must desire such a life.

The prophet Isaiah wrote that there is no other God who "acts for the one who waits for Him." He declared about God: "You meet him who rejoices and does righteousness" (Isa. 64:4–5). If you desire to know God's LifePlan and live it, then He will meet you at the point of your desire. His quick and complete response is for you to discern His LifePlan for you and to grow in it. He sends His Holy Spirit both to give you wisdom to know His will and to enable you to walk in His will.

INVITING THE HOLY SPIRIT TO SPEAK

For nearly three decades, I have helped people discover God's plan and purpose for their lives through a process that I believe the

Lord coached me into developing. It has proven to be a behaviorally and spiritually sound process—a tool for Christians who are willing to invite the Holy Spirit to help them in discernment.

I don't believe you come to a full understanding of yourself through introspection or prayer alone; rather, it is a process that includes dialogue with others. This book provides you with a dialogue of sorts to help you in your self-discovery of God's purpose and plan for your life. In it, you will find questions and exercises aimed at helping you focus on key aspects of your creation.

The help I can offer in a book is not sufficient, however. You will be invited again and again to invite the Holy Spirit to help you see your life more clearly. The Holy Spirit is your steadfast ally in helping you remember the pertinent events of your life, make sense of the data you derive from your life, and assure you that you are discerning clearly God's design and, therefore, God's intent. Bathe your reading of this book in prayer. Your goal is to discover God's higher, divine plan, not simply to work a series of exercises so that you might continue to do what *you* desire to do.

Deuteronomy 28:40 states, "You shall not anoint yourself with the oil." Jesus echoed this truth when He said,

> **The Spirit of the LORD is upon Me,**
> **Because He has anointed Me**
> **To preach the gospel to the poor;**
> **He has sent Me to heal the brokenhearted,**
> **To proclaim liberty to the captives**
> **And recovery of sight to the blind,**
> **To set at liberty those who are oppressed;**
> **To proclaim the acceptable year of the LORD.**
> (Luke 4:18–19)

Jesus did not anoint or empower Himself. The Spirit of God anointed Him and empowered Him to accomplish His mission on earth.

You cannot empower yourself or anoint yourself with God's Spirit. Rather, you must submit yourself to Him to receive His anointing. You must rely on the Holy Spirit for spiritual discernment, and especially discernment about your life. Otherwise, you will tell yourself what you want to hear for selfish ends.

Discernment in Stillness

To hear clearly the voice of the Holy Spirit, you must carve out a space and time for stillness. God speaks most clearly in quietness, stillness. The prophet Elijah certainly knew that. It was only after escaping to a cave, and after spending a night there in solitude and darkness, that Elijah heard God speak (1 Kings 19:9).

I often ask the person who is seeking to know God's LifePlan to come to my mountain home office. There, in the coolness and clean air of the mountains, is an environment of stillness. Our home is in a quiet neighborhood. Many days, the silence is interrupted only by the wind whispering in the tops of the pines that grow in our backyard forest garden.

As you read the following chapters, I encourage you to create for yourself a place of stillness. You may want to wait to read this book until you are alone in your home—perhaps after your family members have gone to bed and you can be assured that you will not be interrupted in your reflection upon the concepts presented here. You may want to take this book with you on a personal retreat to a place where you can be alone, surrounded by God's beautiful creation but uninterrupted by ringing phones or knocks at your door.

God speaks in stillness to hearts that are still. After listening for God in the wind, the rumble of an earthquake, and the roar of a fire, Elijah heard God speak to him "in a still small voice" (1 Kings 19:12). The still small voice was very intimate, very personal—it was "inside" Elijah more than "outside" him. Elijah responded to the voice by wrapping his face in his mantle and walking out of the recesses of the cave to stand at the cave's entrance. There, he heard God speak again.

Your discernment will involve your hearing first in your heart, your spiritual core, the voice of God revealing His desires for you. His voice very likely will not be an audible one, but will be a quiet inner knowing with no less clear a message. Very often I hear a sigh from the person who has sought a LifePlan consultation. One woman began to weep quietly, and as the tears streamed from both eyes, she said very softly, "Oh."

With discernment about what you are to be and do also comes an understanding about what you must do next to grow into your identity and purpose. There is not only discernment of what God intends, but also discernment of what is outside the realm of God's intention. Priorities become very clear once you experience discernment.

A Response Is Required

The response to discernment is yes or no. With discernment comes a choice either to accept or to reject God's LifePlan.

Saying yes to God's LifePlan is inevitably a surrender to God's will, which must include a full surrender to Christ. You come full circle at this point. To know Christ is to enter into a knowing of God's LifePlan. To discern God's LifePlan compels you to desire to know Christ more fully.

A man who came to me for a LifePlan facilitation had faced two realities: (1) he had a six-figure income as a national sales manager, a pressure-packed job, and (2) he was a beeraholic.[2] He invited the Holy Spirit to give him spiritual discernment about his life and what he was to do. In the aftermath of that prayer, this man clearly discerned his future—death within months if he didn't change his ways. He chose life. For him, that decision meant resigning from his job and putting a stop to his drinking. He availed himself of both medical and spiritual help. He entered a different career, one that was challenging to him and had real purpose. Although this man would no doubt have admitted to being under stress and drinking too much, he had to see his life from God's perspective before he would make the changes necessary to truly live the life God meant for him to live. God had given him this revelation before he came to me for a LifePlan. This was essential to saving his life, for at the time he had only months to live if he continued drinking.

Jesus called the Holy Spirit "the Spirit of truth who proceeds from the Father" (John 15:26). The Spirit moves in you continually to testify of Christ Jesus and to enable you to move in the truth. It is your Lord's will that you have to do the asking and searching. When you ask and seek, He responds. His hand moves yours. His mind engages yours. He leads you to the insights through which His plan for you is revealed in all the domains of your life.

Jesus promised His disciples that He would send the Holy Spirit to them for precisely that purpose: to teach them all of the truth of God they needed truly to be God's people, and to comfort, guide, and direct them into all of the paths that God intended for them to walk.

A Prayer for the Holy Spirit's Presence

At the outset of your gaining a new perspective on your life, I strongly encourage you to invite the presence of the Holy Spirit into this process. I've included a prayer that I often use with those who come to me for LifePlans. I invite you to make this prayer your own:

> Guide me. Nudge me. Do not let me go astray. Help me to discern Your will for my life. I cannot accomplish this without Your help. I pray believing that You will be with me in every exercise, and I thank You in advance for helping me. I am not worthy of Your help. It is a great mystery to me that through Your love and grace, You would desire to guide me in this way. But as unworthy as I feel, I also accept Your help and open myself up to it. I thank You and I love You, Holy Spirit, with all of my mind, soul, and spirit.

As you go through each exercise in the remainder of this book, give yourself time to listen quietly to what the Holy Spirit might say to you in your innermost being. Don't hurry the process. Listen in stillness.

AN ONGOING PROCESS

"Living the life" in the title of this book implies process. All doing is done through process. Acts of doing have a beginning, a middle, and an ending. The more effective the process, the more effective the doing and its outcome. The important aspect of process for our purposes is this: *process occurs over time.*

You may not come instantly to every insight necessary for you to live fully the LifePlan God has established for you. In most cases, God reveals Himself to us, and He reveals "us" to us, over time. We grow into an understanding of who we are.

Many people come to me for the LifePlanning process with a sense of frustration and failure about an aspect of their lives. They are quick to blame themselves for missing God's plan for their lives for so many years.

The LifePlanning process is not intended to heap condemnation on you. It is intended to free you, to bring you to a point of awareness so that you might enter more fully into God's plan for your life, and to do so joyously and enthusiastically. While much of the LifePlanning process involves introspection about your present and past, it is truly a forward-moving process. As has been noted by various people through the centuries, the past is prologue. Those without a sense of history are doomed to repeat it. The purpose of the LifePlanning discovery process is to prepare you to make future decisions with greater boldness, clarity, conviction, purpose, and assurance.

A second critical aspect about process is that it rarely is repeatable in minute detail. I have conducted dozens upon dozens of LifePlans, and each process with each person has had a unique quality to it. Some people come to awareness of certain facts about their lives very early in the process, others much later. Some have a very emotional response to their giftedness at one stage of the process, others at another stage.

Remember as you work your way through the exercises in the remainder of this book that these various modules are like threads that are woven together into a tapestry. Each is related to all of the other chapters, but certain chapters are likely to be of greater or lesser benefit to you personally at this time. I have placed the chapters in the sequence that seems to be most productive and beneficial for the majority of people with whom I have worked. Variations are always possible on a good musical theme, and that fact is no less true for this process.

Don't rush to judgment about yourself. Give yourself time to assess the meaning of each exercise. Always strive for breakthrough thinking. Always be open to the Holy Spirit's presence and actively engage in spiritual discernment. Flow with *His* process, in *His* timing.

4

MODULE #1: LIFE DOMAINS AND LIFE SEASONS

The Life Domains are intended to function in balance. Balance is the key to wholeness.

Something has brought you to the point of buying and reading this book. Can you identify it?

You may be experiencing a longing in your heart, perhaps a feeling of being unsettled, unsure, a little confused, frustrated. You may have lost a job or a spouse. You may be entering retirement, or perhaps you are starting out on a career search. These often are times when people reevaluate their lives.

You may be unhappy in a general, unfocused way. You perhaps have taken a long, hard look at your life and said, "I don't like what I see. I want to make changes."

It is important, I believe, that you ask yourself at the outset of the LifePlan process:

- What do I need?
- Why do I feel a desire to read this book?
- What do I hope to gain from revisiting my life?
- Why do I feel the need for a new perspective?

One person came to this process with a long history of marital and vocational failures. She said, "I need to discover what it is that I continue to do wrong. I am not succeeding in my ability to hold together a marriage. I can't seem to hold a job. If I don't discover what I am doing incorrectly, I have a strong sense that I will continue to repeat my mistakes over and over again." She very sadly concluded, "I could die and not ever know why I was to live!"

You may not be in such a desperate state. You may be more like another person, who said to me when he requested that I facilitate a LifePlan for him, "I've had a long string of successes in my life. I have had a good career. I am very pleased with what I have achieved and the work I have done. My wife and I just celebrated our fortieth wedding anniversary. I'm more in love with her than ever. Our children are grown and have successful jobs and marriages. I've always been active in my church and community. But now retirement is staring me in the face, and although I have prepared for this day financially, I am not feeling the least bit prepared for this period of my life emotionally or personally. Frankly I don't *want* to retire. Nevertheless, it's mandatory in my company that I retire by the age of sixty-seven. Please help me discover how I can make the most of the coming years of my life."

When a person comes to me for a LifePlan consultation, my first question is always, "Why are you here?" I ask the person to be as specific and precise as possible. I write down the answer on a large piece of paper so she can see the answer, analyze it, and make any changes she desires. I invite you to make such a statement.

STATEMENT OF EXPECTATION

What I hope to gain from reading this book:

Confirmation and confidence
in God's plan for my life - in

particular the next season of my life -
that I would have COMPLETE peace
and a secure sense of purpose in
getting married.

Take a long, close look at your statement. Evaluate each word. This statement is solely for your purposes so be brutally honest with yourself. Does this statement indicate precisely why you are reading this book? Is it a complete statement? Is it fully accurate? Make any changes you need to make.

Why am I so insistent that you make this statement?

What you hope to gain from something is very often what you *will* gain. You have a perspective as you enter any new experience, be it a conversation, a course, a seminar, or the reading of a book. You come into the experience with a mind-set, a reason for participating, a framework for responding. You need to recognize your mind-set so you may gain the most from the material.

Here are a few sample statements that people have made at the outset of their LifePlan consultations:

- I want to know why I still feel unhappy even though I am doing the job that I always thought I wanted to do.
- I want to know how I can get a better balance in my life between work and family.
- I want to feel less stress.
- I want to know why I seem to keep making the same mistakes over and over again.
- I want to discover God's plan for me in my retirement years.

These statements are diverse. The people who made them were at very different places in their personal and vocational lives. And the fact is, what the people eventually got out of the LifePlanning process was very different—each had a different reason for entering the process; therefore, each had a different way of approaching each exercise in the process. The person who was seeking less stress, for example, looked at his life in a quite different way from that of the person who was looking for clues about what might make for a good retirement plan.

If you want to maximize your success, say so. Define what success is for you.

If you want to solve problems, say so. Be precise about which problems.

If you want insight into the unknown, say so. What unknowns concern you most?

In identifying what you want, you establish a foundation upon which to receive. Ask for what you want with belief, supplication, and thanksgiving.

WHAT DO YOU WANT GOD TO DO FOR YOU?

I have always been rather amazed at the story of blind Bartimaeus in the Bible. There he stood, in every way a blind man. He was dressed in the way blind beggars dressed at that time. He no doubt used a walking stick as a blind man's cane. His eyes did not focus. And yet Jesus said to him, standing face-to-face with him, "What do you want Me to do for you?" (See Mark 10:46–52.)

To all around Jesus, the question must have seemed as if Jesus were asking the obvious. And yet Jesus was very precise in His question. He certainly knew what Bartimaeus *needed* and *desired,* for the Scriptures also tell us that Jesus knew fully what was in each person's heart. (See John 2:25.) Jesus asked that question so that Bartimaeus might be confronted with his own answer.

The broader question being asked of you at the outset is not solely what you desire from the reading of this book, but what you want out of your life. How do you want your life to be different? What do you wish for yourself? What are your desires, dreams, hopes—many of which may be secret, long buried, or never fully explored?

Bartimaeus replied, "I want my sight." And Jesus gave his sight to him. When you can say clearly to God and to yourself, "This is truly what I want," I believe that nearly always is *precisely* what God gives to you, although the process of His giving and your receiving His gift may not happen as quickly as it happened for Bartimaeus.

Much responsibility fell on Bartimaeus the instant he received his sight. The encounter with Jesus was a life-changing experience for him. Bartimaeus from that point on would be required to earn a living, not beg for one. He would be required to do many things for himself that he had previously not been required to do. He would be responsible for reading and studying the Torah, the Law of God, for himself—no more secondhand information. He would be responsible for keeping the feasts and rituals of the Jewish religion, some of which he had been prohibited from doing previously. In saying, "I want my sight," Bartimaeus was also saying, "I want a new life."

Do you want a completely new life? Do you want a greatly amended life? Are you willing to make the changes that a LifePlan might indicate? Are you willing to accept a new perspective on your life?

I believe God asks each of us, "What do you want Me to do for you?"

Yet another point I want to bring to your attention is that Bartimaeus *really* wanted what he wanted. He cried out with a loud voice to get Jesus' attention. The Bible tells us that the more he called out to Jesus, the more the disciples and others told him to keep his peace. Bartimaeus refused to heed their admonitions. He cried out to Jesus all the louder.

What you receive in life is largely a result of how much you ardently want to receive what you pursue. I could point to any number of people who may not have a great deal of talent, but they have worked at the talent they do have and they have continued to push and push and push, with intensity, toward a goal, and they have succeeded in reaching far greater heights than an equal number of people who are highly talented and not at all motivated to pursue a goal or develop their talents.

Do you *really* want what you have said you want? How much do you want this change?

So often people give lip service to change. They say they want to lead a new life or to follow a new path, but in reality, they find it much more comfortable to stay in their old rut. Do you *really* want to discover God's LifePlan for you? Do you *really* want to know your reason for being? Are you willing to pursue that reason for being with the utmost of your energy and with a complete focus?

Take one final look at your reason-for-reading statement. What does it say about you to you?

LIFE IS A WHOLE WITH MANY PARTS

We can point to various roles or functions that we fill in life. Life has categories; it is a whole with many parts. Although none of us can segment ourselves, we can take an objective look at different aspects of our lives in order to see how they relate to other aspects as well as how they relate to the whole.

The term I give to these facets of life is *Life Domains:*

- *Personal*—this is the domain of the self.
- *Family*—this domain includes parents, spouse, children, and influential extended family members.
- *Church/faith kingdom*—this is the domain in which a person relates to others within the body of Christ.
- *Vocation*—this is the domain of work or career, including areas of volunteer service for which one has responsibility.
- *Community*—this is the domain in which a person gives back to the society at large; community may be one's church, but it is usually one's neighborhood, town, or city.

If you do not live a balanced, focused life in each of these five domains, you cannot fully succeed in carrying out God's LifePlan.

Several principles related to the Life Domains are critical:

Each domain impacts all others. If a person is experiencing failure in family life, for example, he will bring his overall life imbalance to his vocation. Deep within, he will feel like a failure; his failure complex will be like a fog permeating his personal life. He will find it nearly impossible to accept acclaim or experience joy. In like manner, if a person is not growing personally, she will find it very difficult to help her community grow in positive ways. If a person is struggling in his vocation, his family will feel the results. And so on. Each area is one in which to seek growth and strength so that the whole might be made stronger.

Very often we fail to understand how important the various domains are to one another. Many people, for example, do not realize the impact made on an entire life—as well as on an entire family, an entire church, an entire community—when a person loses a job.

Thirty percent of our white-collar workforce in the United States has been downsized from corporations in the last ten years. Some of the people are living in sheer desperation in a state that I call permanently temporarily unemployed. In our American culture, we define ourselves to a great extent by our jobs. Women have said to me, "I'm just a housewife"—some proudly and some bitterly. Men have said to me, "I'm a manager in my company, an engineer by training." Both statements are self-definitions according to the *work* a person does or the functional role the person fills.

We are also creatures of comparison. We place more value on supervisors than on line workers. We look up to leaders and have little regard for followers. As part of our ability to relate to another person, we seek to know a person's position or ranking.

When someone loses a job, she loses a significant percentage of her self-definition. The unemployed person no longer knows how to regard herself, or how to relate to the broader society. Her self-esteem, finances, family life, sense of purpose and direction, ability to set goals and make plans, and her feelings of value and worth all have been shaken to the core.

To a great extent, she doesn't know who she is or how she fits. And most of all, she no longer feels whole. Although we segment the five Life Domains for the purpose of examining our lives and gaining understanding, the reality is that we cannot completely compartmentalize or isolate any Life Domain. They interconnect at all levels of existence—conscious, subconscious, emotional, physical.

The five domains are not necessarily equal. A person may not be able to donate as much time or energy, for example, to the community domain as to the vocation or family domain. Nevertheless, the community domain is a vital part of the whole. It cannot be totally neglected for a person to be whole.

The five domains are not rigid. In some cases, one or more of these domains may be combined. Many pastors have difficulty separating church/faith kingdom and vocation. The two domains function as one in their lives.

At times, a person may have so many close family ties that he says, "My community is my family; my family is my community." If that is the case, the two domains are combined.

In a few cases, a person has convinced me that the church/faith kingdom and community function as one in her life. The neighborhood church may be both neighborhood and church.

A mother who stays at home with her children may choose to combine family and vocation domains.

The personal domain, however, must not be combined with other domains. It is very important that a person not eliminate or subsume his personal expression under any other domain.

That does not mean, of course, that in some instances, a person's vocation and personal life may not be very closely aligned. I met a woman who loves to read, write, and travel. These would usually be expressions of the personal domain. However, she makes her living as a writer, a career that involves both travel and research (mostly reading).

I encouraged her to classify in the vocation domain any interest that was in some way related to her work. In the personal domain she left her love of music and her hobby of needlework.

The key to the five domains is balance. Every person will have a slightly different balance point for the five Life Domains.

Many highly successful people are out of balance, and very often, the balance is skewed toward vocation. Personal and family life suffer, as do commitments to church and community.

Generally speaking, you will have an intuitive understanding when things are balanced or "right" in your life or when something is out of balance. A lack of balance creates an inner tension, which you may perceive as a nagging stress, a feeling of frustration, or a sensation that something important is missing or lacking.

> ***When Jesus saw him lying there, and knew that he already had been in that condition a long time, He said to him, "Do you want to be made well?"*** (John 5:6)

THE CORE IS CHRIST

A living core is necessary if you are to keep the five Life Domains in balance. For the Christian, that living core is Christ Jesus. He is the unifying, integrating force.

Every symphony has a leitmotiv—a set of notes forming a dominant theme that repeats itself in various forms throughout each of the symphony's movements. For the Christian, Christ is the leitmotiv. He exerts His presence, His "theme song," in every area of your life. The individual embellishments on His core presence are the result of your personality and unique giftedness.

Metapoint is a nautical term describing the point where a line passing through the center of a boat intersects with a line passing through the center of gravity. I have a client, E. Paul Casey, who is a sailor and who has built a company on the metapoint concept—he acquires a company and then, with the assistance of a team of top executives that includes investor-partners, builds it up to a point of financial buoyancy, selling the company several years later at a high multiple on earnings. Christianity is all about metapoint—about coming to the place where we overcome evil and the tug of the world against us and become buoyant in our joy in Christ Jesus.

When I worked as an aerospace weight engineer, I spent much of my time in determining the exact center of gravity for any design. One must determine the center of gravity if a design is to be balanced and to function properly. God desires for each of us to have Christ as our center of gravity. He is the One who calls us to a balanced life so that we might function properly in the role to which we are called.

Whether you relate to the analogy of leitmotiv, metapoint, or center of gravity, Christ must be central to your life. In diagram form, the Life Domains may look like this:

LIFE DOMAINS

The Most Important Life Domain: Personal

The personal domain is always the most important. If it is not centered on or grounded in Christ, all of the other domains will be on shaky ground. Ask yourself these questions:

- Am I truly centered on Christ and His commandments and teachings?

- Do I believe in myself? Am I secure in my worth as a unique human being?
- Am I placing relationships before tasks, specifically, family before vocation?
- Have I accepted my giftedness, and am I serving God out of it?
- Am I striving for a balance in all of the Life Domains, and trusting God to give me the miracle of His grace as I attempt to find and maintain this balance?
- Do I see myself in a state of continually becoming more Christlike? Am I aware that Christ is actualizing His life in me?
- Am I holding myself accountable to Christ Jesus—the Author, Perfecter, and Finisher of my identity and my destiny?

Relationship to Church/Faith Kingdom

The personal domain is the area of personal faith. In contrast, the church/faith kingdom domain is the area of affiliation that you have with other believers. You may have a strong affiliation with other Christians through prayer groups, Bible study fellowships, home fellowship groups, and so forth. You may be in church leadership and find that your affiliation in the church is stronger with your ministerial peers than it is with members of your congregation (who are perceived more as part of your vocation). However you define church/faith kingdom is up to you. Nevertheless, the core of your faith in Jesus Christ belongs in the personal realm. Your faith in Him is something you take with you regardless of where you attend church or with whom you share Christ.

The Realm of Your Desires and Longings

In the personal realm, I have had people try repeatedly to move the topic of discussion to their families or to their churches or businesses. The reason is usually that they are very uncomfortable with the idea of doing something pleasurable solely for themselves. They generally have had very little experience in loving themselves—giving themselves special treats, doing things they want to do, enjoying things they like. I sometimes ask, "What would you do if God told you that you had a day or weekend to do anything *you* like to do—just as God's special reward to you?"

One man said he would spend the entire day reading Civil War history. That wouldn't be much fun for me, but it was an ideal self-indulgent day to him. He voiced his choice in cautious terms, as if I thought a minister of the gospel shouldn't want to read Civil War history. He had been fascinated with the Civil War since he was in junior high school. "Why not spend a day that way occasionally?" I asked.

"Oh, I'm much too busy. It's not something that is important to God's work."

"But it is," I said. "It's a desire that you have in your heart and that is important to God. It's an avenue for Him to teach you certain lessons He desires to teach you. And beyond that, God delights in what delights you. Just as you take pleasure in what causes your little girl to squeal with delight, so God takes pleasure in what brings a smile to your face. Doing what pleases you is a means of saying to God, 'This is the way You made me, and I like the way You made me.'"

I knew from the expression on his face that he had never thought of his appreciation for Civil War history in those terms. He told me later, "You are the first person who ever gave me permission to do some of the things I like to do. You are the only one who has given me permission really to be *me*."

You are a mixture of desires, longings, hopes, and dreams. The doing of things that give you happiness, pleasure, and exhilaration is vital to your being a whole person. When you deny the personal domain, you deny God access to a major area of your being. You close off a part of yourself that He desires to redeem, develop, and use.

What Aren't You Giving to Yourself?

When we deal with the personal domain, I generally ask, "What aren't you giving to yourself?"

This is an especially difficult question for pastors to answer. After he had pondered this question for several minutes, one pastor said, "This is tough, Tom. This is tough."

When you fail to love yourself, you fail to give God credit for what He has done in you and for you.

Those who are involved in full-time ministerial careers—as well as those who are Christian social workers, psychologists, counselors, and others in helping professions—very often are so immersed in assisting others that they never take time for themselves. In some cases, they have been taught—incorrectly, in my opinion—to believe that they should never be concerned for themselves. They are self-martyrs, although they almost always fail to recognize that they are requiring far more of themselves than God requires.

Jesus gave these great commandments: "'You shall love the LORD your God with all your heart, with all your soul, and with all your mind.' This is the first and great commandment. And the second is like it: 'You shall love your neighbor as yourself.' On these two commandments hang all the Law and the Prophets" (Matt. 22:37–40).

Love your neighbor *as yourself.* If you don't love yourself, you have no foundation on which to build love for your neighbor. God doesn't expect you to hate yourself and love your neighbor. He expects you to love yourself and, out of that love, to love your neighbor.

Why is it so important that you love yourself? Because loving yourself is appreciating who God made you to be. It's an act of praise and worship to love yourself because in so doing, you are acknowledging that God is a masterful Creator! He made you just the way you are. He loves you to the point that He sent His only begotten Son, Jesus Christ, to die on the cross in your place so that you might receive forgiveness for your sins, be reconciled to God the Father, and live with God forever in heaven. When you fail to love yourself, you fail to give God credit for what He has done in you and for you.

When you fail to love yourself, you close yourself off from being a vessel through whom God can work. You "shut down" some of the ways in which God might use you under the guise of saying,

"I'm not worthy. I'm not good enough. I'm not capable. I'm not useful in this area." Who are you to say you can't when God has created you for that very purpose?

The person who loves herself is a person who says, "God made me the way I am, so I am pleasing to Him; therefore, I must be highly valuable and useful and lovable. God loved me so much that Jesus died for my sins. God wants to live with me throughout all eternity, so He must consider me to be very special in His eyes. I am His beloved child. God desires to pour His Holy Spirit through me to others so that I might be a blessing on this earth, and if God desires to dwell in me and use me, then I am a valuable asset in His kingdom. I am a child of God. I am loved with an infinite unconditional love."

When a person sees himself as a beloved child of God, a forgiven son, a minister of God's grace to others, that person is fully capable of loving others, for he will see every person he encounters as someone God loves. He will see every person as worthy of God's forgiveness. He will see every person as a potential for blessing under the guidance and empowerment of the Holy Spirit.

Until you love yourself, you cannot love others *as Christ loves them*. You can talk about God's love to them. You can tell them about God's laws and commandments. You can give them God's plan of salvation. But you can't really and truly love them with a heartfelt love.

Nurturing the Self

Love for self will manifest itself as nurture of the self. This often comes in the form of play or recreation.

You need to have activities as part of your daily, weekly, and annual schedule that are exclusively for the feeding of your personality, desires, and dreams. For one young man I know, this activity is fishing. He takes two or three fishing trips a year—trout fishing in the mountains, deep-sea fishing off Baja California. These trips are his opportunity to rejuvenate, to relax, and to feed a part of himself that is very important to his ability to perform in his job and to take on family, church, and community activities the remainder of the year.

Fishing is a positive, healthy, vital part of his life. He doesn't carry this activity to the point where it negatively impacts his family and their life together.

Unfortunately his wife and children did not understand the value of this personal time. His wife resented his participation in an activity that seems to exclude her. In the wake of her bitter resentment, he had come to feel guilty about going fishing. In his guilt, he had become frustrated and confused, and he felt resentful in return.

Once he realized that the fishing trips were vital for the health and well-being of his personhood—and that they were truly one of the things that were *right* about his personal life—he felt freedom and affirmation. He also had a new foundation on which he might explain his love for fishing to his wife. "God made me to be a fisherman," he said proudly. "That's part of who I am! When I don't express my fisherman nature, I'm not taking full care of the personal identity that God gave me."

The more he talked about himself as a fisherman, the more he saw the truth about his makeup. He was able to gain a new perspective on the way he dealt with other issues in his life, and he had a new understanding of the way he processed information and made decisions. Embracing his passion for fishing gave him an entry point for embracing much about himself that he had previously questioned or denied. His wife came to understand this and realized that she, too, had personal needs that, because they were unfulfilled, were stunting her life. Now they are supporting each other's personal needs and, not surprisingly, their marriage is better than ever.

Winston Churchill carried a union card for the Bricklayer's Union his entire life. He laid bricks regardless of other positions he held and the world prominence he achieved. He said on a number of occasions that he enjoyed laying bricks because it was an activity in which he didn't have to think. I've seen the brickwork that he did at his home in England. He did excellent work! Bricklaying was a personal outlet for him.

Churchill also painted. That was his second outlet for relaxation. He painted regardless of the wartime pressures that confronted him relentlessly—in fact, he painted because of them. Churchill knew that a person needs an outlet for fun to relieve stress and that the result of healthy recreation is nearly always an increase in physical, emotional, intellectual, and spiritual strength, and a broadening or freshening of perspective.

Even in war, a soldier has R and R breaks for rest and relaxation. Yet how many people in the business world, who fight daily battles of an intense emotional nature, fail to give themselves adequate R and R? They feel guilty for taking time off. They apologize for needing vacation breaks.

Personal fun and recreation are part of God's design for your life. The personal domain is no less important than any other domain in your fulfillment of God's plan and purposes. Having a strong personal domain is vital to your being whole.

Someone who chooses a service profession—such as a pastor, counselor, or social worker—must recognize that he is making a career decision that will impact the amount of time available for a personal life and a family life. To a great extent, a service profession within the church structure—such as pastor—spans the domains of church, community, and vocation. If such a person is to have a healthy personal and family life, he will have to make very intentional efforts to plan for it, and he will have to be very diligent in maintaining his plan.

STATING OBJECTIVES IN THE FIVE LIFE DOMAINS

After a person has identified his or her overall objective in pursuing a LifePlan, I ask the person to identify specific subgoals or subobjectives for each of the five Life Domains: personal, family, vocation, church/faith kingdom, and community. These statements need not mirror, but they should harmonize with, the general objective or goal statement.

State for yourself specific objectives in each domain:

YOUR OBJECTIVE STATEMENTS

GENERAL OBJECTIVE STATEMENT *(your previous goal statement)*:

____

____

____

____

PERSONAL	
FAMILY	
CHURCH/ FAITH KINGDOM	
VOCATION	
COMMUNITY	

Now take a look at your six objective statements—your general statement and specific Life Domain statements. See them as a whole. Do you have a strong sense of what you *need* in your life at this present time?

Understanding your needs is an important first step in gaining perspective on your life. You are likely to see significant overlap or relationship in the statements and thus gain insight into the greater whole of your needs. This usually happens when you pair a goal or need statement for a particular domain with the general statement, or pair two specific goal/need statements. What might you conclude from these two sample statements?

General	**Personal Domain**
To discover ways to lower a nagging sense of frustration in my life.	To discover ways to improve my general health and spiritual well-being.

As a facilitator for LifePlans, I might draw two conclusions:

1. The person's nagging sense of frustration may be caused by something that is wrong with her physically or spiritually.
2. This person's peace may improve as she takes steps to improve her general health and spiritual well-being.

Consider for a moment that this same hypothetical person had stated as a goal/need statement in the vocation domain: "Discover ways to streamline my work so that I am more efficient."

I might conclude as a facilitator that inefficiency and wasted motion in this person's vocation may be contributing to her frustration and also to her poor physical and spiritual health.

Do you see how these statements may combine and interrelate to give you even more meaning than is apparent in each statement taken on its own merit?

As you review your objective statements for pursuing the Life-Planning process, what are your initial insights?

THE SEASONS OF YOUR LIFE

Just as life has several domains, so life has seasons. Your roles and functions in each Life Domain change with the seasons. The seasons are like those in nature:

• *Winter—early youth.* These are the years in which the soil of your life is prepared to receive information and to acquire skills. Your parents give you a foundation of esteem, value, and worthiness. They teach you language and model values for you. You internalize the framework you will carry with you all your life.

• *Spring—education/preparation years.* These are the school and college or vocational training years in which you acquire skills and information. Valuable seeds are planted in you.

• *Summer—work years.* These are the long, tedious, exhilarating, intense years of working at your craft and developing your giftedness. You continue to grow in skills and information, but much of your effort is directed toward *doing.*

• *Harvest—later years.* These are the golden years of reaping from what you have sown. These are also the years of giving and sharing what you are reaping.

> ***To everything there is a season, A time for every purpose under heaven.*** (Eccl. 3:1)

Part of facing your future lies in recognizing the season of life in which you are living. A man came to me for a LifePlan consultation as he was facing retirement from a company he had led for a number of years. He had turned the company around from financial loss to considerable profit. Over a long career, he had turned around several companies. He thought he might spend his retirement years consulting with companies that were in trouble. In fact, he had received several offers to enter into such consulting contracts. He had even considered the possibility of taking another position that would be short-term but full-time. His name is Jim Buick, and he was retiring as CEO of Zondervan Publishing.

I asked Jim, "Which season of life are you in?" I explained to him the concept of seasons of life, and he finally said, "I'm in the autumn years. I'm sixty-one. It's time I reap the rewards of my years of hard work. I don't have anything I need to prove or any opponents to conquer. I want these to be *giving* years, not earning years."

In the first three months following his LifePlan consultation, Jim turned down three offers to turn around sick companies. He did it without hesitation because they didn't fit the plan. He told this to Max DePree, a friend and former chairman of Herman Miller Corporation. Max replied simply, "Autumn is a wonderful time of life, Jim."

Activities Change "Seasonally"

You have been shaped and fashioned for a specific mission, but this mission changes from season to season in your life. Your giftedness does not change, but its *application* has phases. These phases are as much a part of God's creative process in you as any other aspect of your being.

I am a designer. As a trained systems engineer, I am capable of designing products as well as strategies and processes. I have manifested my design gifts in each of these ways. But I also have designed a formal Japanese garden in my backyard. All of my designs flow from the gift of design that God has placed in me.

I am very aware that at specific times in my life, my gift of design was intended by God to be manifested in certain ways, and at other times in my life, that gift was to be manifested in different ways. The application of the gift changed; the gift itself did not.

For several decades I applied my gift of designing strategies—my gift of planning—to helping companies and corporations. Now I apply my gift primarily to helping individuals, many of whom work in churches or have a deep interest in becoming more Christlike. The gift has not changed in me, other than that it has grown and developed. The application of the gift has changed considerably.

You must be aware constantly in the LifePlan process that God may desire that you apply your giftedness in a way that is different from the way you have applied it in the past. Allow yourself the flexibility of moving to a new season in your life and of adjusting your objectives for each Life Domain to reflect your current season.

You *are* who you are.

What you *do* may change considerably.

Reevaluate your Life Domain statements in the light of the current season of your life. Are your objectives appropriate for the season in which you find yourself? Make whatever adjustments are necessary.

WHAT INSIGHTS DO YOU HAVE?

At this point, you may want to note a few insights that you are beginning to have about your life.

- Is your life in balance? If not, what areas may need to be brought into balance?
- Is Christ Jesus truly at the core of your life?
- Are your current objectives in line with your season of life?
- In what ways are you gaining a new perspective on yourself?

5

MODULE #2: FOUR HELPFUL LISTS

No one has ever criticized a person to success,
and all of us are masters of self-criticism.
We need no help in that department!
Jesus modeled the path to realizing potential:
the encouraging word, hope, affirmation,
and validation.
He wants us to believe in ourselves,
to love ourselves, as unconditionally as He does.

I don't rely on any of the current, commonly used diagnostic tools employed by psychologists and career planning counselors. They are good ones, and I have used them in the past in my larger consulting practice when I had a business unit devoted to recruitment. The standard diagnostic tools, however, generally are an end unto themselves; they are not an integral part of helping persons see their total giftedness and call to service.

The LifePlan diagnostic tools have been designed specifically for the LifePlan process. They have proven to work well in providing people with a perspective that leads naturally and directly into a recognition of their LifePlan.

In the previous chapter, I asked you to provide objective statements related to your Life Domains. Now we move directly into these diagnostic modules:

- Four Helpful Lists
- Turning Points Profile
- Talent Search
- Drivers and Comfort Zones
- Thinking Wavelength
- Transformation Through Surrender

As we approach each of these, I will present the construct in its entirety, explain each portion of it to you, and then invite you to complete the construct for yourself. Everything that has been discussed about gaining perspective, especially about breakthrough thinking and spiritual discernment, should be related to the material in these upcoming chapters.

FOUR HELPFUL QUESTIONS

The four helpful lists are derived from four questions that I believe are at the heart of helping you gain perspective about where you are in your life right now. Peter Drucker asks the leadership team of a business to ask themselves such questions relative to their business. They apply to an individual life as well. Here are the questions:

1. *What is right about your life?*
2. *What is wrong about your life?*
3. *What is confused in your life?*
4. *What is missing from your life?*

Each of these questions is then applied to the Life Domains in a matrix format:

THE FOUR HELPFUL LISTS MATRIX

LIFE DOMAINS	What Is Right? (optimize)	What Is Wrong? (change)	What Is Confused? (clarify)	What Is Missing? (add)
PERSONAL				
FAMILY				
CHURCH/ FAITH KINGDOM				
VOCATION				
COMMUNITY				

WHAT IS RIGHT?

Identifying what is right in your life gives you perspective on what you might *optimize* in the future.

One of the most rationed resources in our world today is affirmation. There is a general tendency on the part of virtually every person I meet not to believe in self.

At every point possible, I attempt to affirm those with whom I work. I challenge you to address your life with a positive viewpoint. Recognize what a wonderful, good, creative, intelligent, and talented person you are!

> *The LORD will perfect that which concerns me;*
> *Your mercy, O LORD, endures forever;*
> *Do not forsake the works of Your hands.*
> (Ps. 138:8)

Great Human Qualities

Some of the great human qualities, manifested in every person I know, are these:

We need to grow. We need to be free to modify, to change, and to become what we can become.

We can trust and be trusted. Trust relationships take time, but we are able to trust. Mutual help depends on trust environments.

We are creative. We experience a sense of supreme well-being and gratification when thinking through how to do things better.

We want to do good work. We take pride in accomplishments. As children we all insisted, "Look at me." We have a built-in desire for applause. It is natural for us to do our best, and it is natural for us to require and demand recognition.

We manage ourselves. Each person has a basic sense of independence that makes him or her a self-manager. It is part of our survival instinct.

We want to learn. It is innate in each of us that we must learn. Our survival and progress as human beings depend on this programmed-in animating force.

We challenge ourselves. We self-actualize. In fact, we can do this only for ourselves. No one can do it for us. No one can drive us to it.

We voluntarily take risks. Behavioral studies have proven repeatedly that we will voluntarily assume a thousand times more risk than can be imposed on us against our will.

We need to belong. Deep within each of us is the necessity, the longing, to belong. Coals burn longest in the fire. Set one on the hearth and it is soon cold. The same is true for human beings. Families and circles of friends nourish the spirit.

Far Beyond a Human Resource

I loathe the term *human resource;* I consider it dehumanizing. It's one of the greatest insults ever perpetuated upon a person who has a corporate or manufacturing vocation. I have never met a person who has said to me, "I am a human resource." No! Each person is a unique being, a person created in the image of God. Each person has human qualities that other types of resources do not have. (See Eph. 2:10.)

The human resource mind-set does not exist only in the vocational world, of course. Parents often have the same mind-set toward their children—just feed and clothe and provide for them until they are adults. "Get them to adulthood and hope for the best" is the philosophy of too many parents. Pastors and church leaders have this mind-set when they think in terms of their parish or congregation rather than of individuals who are hurting and in spiritual and emotional need. Teachers and other professionals have this mind-set when they classify those over whom they have authority as a class, clients, patients, or customers rather than as human beings with legitimate talents, desires, dreams, goals, and other positive qualities.

Anytime you see yourself as part of a class of people, rather than as a unique individual with unlimited potential, you demean yourself. In the process, you put a cap on your productivity and achievement. You begin to adopt the stance emotionally, "I can't or I won't be able to or I shouldn't because I am a ______________." Fill in the blank with any stereotype or group classification you desire. The result is the same.

Today is the day to affirm yourself as a person who has a need to grow, can trust and be trusted, is never more in flow than when being creative, wants to do good work and to learn, is capable of managing yourself and challenging yourself, is willing to assume great risks, and has a wonderful need to belong and to build trust relationships with other people. You are somebody special. You are a creation of the almighty Creator.

WHAT IS WRONG?

This question produces a list of things that might be corrected. Little needs to be said about this question or the lists that result. Most people are very aware of what they believe to be wrong with their lives, but they have never stated it aloud to themselves. This is the opportunity to declare it in order to fix it. Keep in mind that this is a question intended to produce a list of what might be *changed.* Very few wrongs are permanent in nature. God's work is one of redemption, forgiveness, and renewal.

WHAT IS CONFUSED?

Most people have an area of their lives that is in a state of confusion or that they believe needs to be prioritized, organized, refocused, or discerned more clearly. The answer to this question gives you a chance to *clarify.*

In identifying what is confused, you readily admit to yourself that you don't know if something is right or wrong, true or false. You need more information to bring the issue or question to closure. Identification of the confusion in your life points you toward what you need to learn, discover, examine more closely, or put to the test.

WHAT IS MISSING?

Where are the voids? The answer points toward what might be *added* in your life.

The voids tend to be just outside your field of inner vision. You may have a feeling that something is uncertain, unknown, unsettled. You may not even be able to articulate fully the nature of the void. In some cases, the entire domain may appear to be a void.

I once hosted a pastor for a LifePlan session, and as we discussed the Four Helpful Lists Matrix, he said to me, "I don't know what you mean by the personal domain." I gave him a very general definition, and he still responded, "I'm not sure what you mean." I discussed the domain with him further, yet he still seemed confused.

I realized that he truly didn't have a personal life, and he hadn't had one for so many years that he had lost all concept of what it meant to have a personal life. He didn't do anything that was "just for him." He had no personal dreams or goals. His entire life had become oriented toward serving others and, to a great extent, living up to their expectations. No wonder he sat before me confused and feeling drained and frustrated. All sense of personal life had been extracted from him by the demands of others. For him, the entire column under "Personal" yielded very little information.

When we confronted the fact that an entire domain of his life was missing, he was well on his way toward having a perspective that could yield very positive decisions about his immediate future.

Since you do not have the benefit of a facilitator to help you see the voids in your life, it is especially important that you invite the Holy Spirit to speak to you. Ask Him to reveal to you what you are missing.

A SUMMARY OF THE FOUR HELPFUL QUESTIONS

The four helpful questions are intended to direct you toward positive growth and change. Let me briefly summarize that goal for you:

Question	**Direction**
RIGHT?	OPTIMIZED
WRONG?	CORRECTED, CHANGED
CONFUSED?	CLARIFIED
MISSING?	ADDED

The answers to these questions are placed on a matrix of the five Life Domains. As you work your way through this matrix, keep these points in mind:

• *Deal with only one domain at a time.* For example, answer the "What is right?" question across all five Life Domains—personal, family, church/faith kingdom, vocation, community—before moving on to the "What is wrong?" question.

• *Identify only one item for each question.* Don't try to take on more than one item. If you do, you will feel mentally and emotionally self-defeated. Focus on the one thing that is most right, most wrong, most confused, and most absent.

Now, complete the matrix on pages 88–89, giving yourself sufficient time for reflection and inviting the Holy Spirit to reveal to you *His* answers.

Here is a quick review of the domains for your reference as you work on the matrix:

- *Personal*—your personal health, emotions, mind, possessions, and general well-being.
- *Family*—your immediate and extended family, including parents, spouse, children, and other close familial relationships.
- *Church/faith kingdom*—your church or the broader faith community in which you are a member.
- *Vocation*—your career or work life, including volunteer work and tasks for which you are regularly responsible.
- *Community*—your neighborhood, city, or other defined community in which you are a member.

RECOGNIZING CONTROLLABILITY

To get a true picture that reflects potential for growth or change, you must have some understanding of the controllability that you have over the answers or issues raised. In nearly all cases, you will have at least partial controllability over the ability to optimize, change, clarify, or fill a void. You must recognize your ability to alter circumstances you do not like and to build on those you do like.

Controllability is rated as "full," "partial," or "none." In some cases, you may not be able to control a circumstance. For example, you may have a physical condition, you may lose a loved one, or your life and family may have been hit by a natural tragedy that has caused an irreplaceable loss. Keep in mind, however, that your *response* to this situation may give you some control over the overall situation. A loss of a job may be what's wrong, perhaps even what is missing; you may have had no control at all over the loss of the job, but you do have control over the situation of being jobless.

Situations involving other people are nearly always situations in which you have only partial control. Situations in which you alone are involved are nearly always situations in which you have full control.

Review this sample form, using F for full controllability, P for partial controllability, and N for no controllability.

SAMPLE
PERSONAL DOMAIN

	CONTROLLABILITY
What is right? (Chance to Optimize)	
In career that I enjoy	P
What is wrong? (Chance to Change)	
Lack of confidence in talents	F
What is confused? (Chance to Clarify)	
Multiple opportunities that need to be prioritized	P
What is missing? (Chance to Fill Voids)	
Social life needs to be improved	P

Return to your Four Helpful Lists Matrix and add an F, P, or N to each cell.

THE FOUR HELPFUL LISTS MATRIX

LIFE DOMAINS	What Is Right? (optimize)	What Is Wrong? (change)
(Only one item should be stated in each cell.)		
PERSONAL		
FAMILY		
CHURCH/ FAITH KINGDOM		
VOCATION		
COMMUNITY		

LIFE DOMAINS	What Is Confused? (clarify)	What Is Missing? (add)

(Only one item should be stated in each cell.)

PERSONAL		
FAMILY		
CHURCH/ FAITH KINGDOM		
VOCATION		
COMMUNITY		

WHAT INSIGHTS DO YOU HAVE?

At this point, you may want to note a few insights that you are beginning to have about your life.

Take a look at your four helpful lists as a *whole*. Move to a higher level of thinking, a broader perspective. Circle two or three areas that you believe may be critical for immediate action. You may see that an alteration in just one or two areas—perhaps bringing resolution to something that is wrong, confused, or missing, or by enhancing something that is right—positively impacts several other areas. If you have full controllability in the most critical areas you have circled, you have the opportunity for immediate and effective change or growth—you have leverage. Take courage, take charge, and take action!

Reflect for a few moments on how your completion of the Four Helpful Lists Matrix relates to the objectives you wrote in Chapter 4.

Which of the points of your personal domain would help most to lift your personal life to a new level if you were to focus on them? Leverage isn't always necessary in correcting a wrong. A change can be created by optimizing a right or in filling a void.

In what ways are you starting to gain a new perspective on your life?

6

MODULE #3: THE TURNING POINTS PROFILE

Part 1 Identifying and Charting Your Turning Points

The Turning Points Profile is the most important construct I use to help people gain perspective. For most of the people with whom I facilitate LifePlans, this is the most careful and thorough introspection they have ever made of their lives.

A charting of turning points is the major construct in the LifePlanning process to help you gain perspective on your life. The end result of a turning point survey is a time line, of sorts, for your life.

A turning point is a point when the direction of your life changes, for better or worse. The previous pattern or trend is not continued. Something intervenes, occurs, or is decided that alters the future course.

HALLMARKS OF A TURNING POINT

A turning point is an inflection point on your life journey. You see them as you look back on your history, asking questions such as these:

- What was happening during this period of my life? What set the tone for that period? What decision or event led me into that period of my life? What decision or event marked the end of that period?
- What marked the beginning or ending of a stage that I went through?
- What change resulted from the tragedy or crisis that I experienced?
- What were the major moments in which I experienced great joy or fulfillment?
- What are the major events of my life (such as marriage, death, leaving home, divorce, graduation, career shifts, retirement)?

Milestones

One way to approach turning points is to regard them as significant milestones in life. A milestone is a significant event in one's progress or developing. We routinely use this term throughout our culture. For example, we say, "His getting that job was a milestone in his career," or "Her conversion was a milestone—everybody could see the transformation in her life."

The Future Is Different from the Past

The future is *not* the same as the past once you have passed through a turning point. In looking back, you see that you were moving in a certain direction, then something happened that altered your course and changed your life in some way. Certain things of the past may have been dropped or significantly altered; other things may have been strengthened or emphasized.

A turning point is not necessarily an event, although that may be the case, such as a spiritual conversion, a marriage or divorce, a death in the family. At times a turning point is the natural transition from one stage of life to the next, such as when you go away to college or begin a new career.

In charting turning points, you look for periods of time and key events that can be pretty much isolated and defined as units of time.

Let's consider John Baker again. He was the national sales manager, earning a six-figure income, who one day felt his liver, and it was as hard as a rock. He went to his physician who told him, "You have two months, or perhaps six months, unless you change your ways. It's up to you." He faced a fully controllable decision at that point.

That event marked a turning point in his life. He quit his sales manager job, gave up the high income, stopped drinking, entered a twelve-step recovery program, became a pastor, and wrote a Christ-centered twelve-step book that has been of significant benefit to many who have drinking or substance-abuse problems and their families.

The turning point was facing a liver disease and responding to it in a Christ-focused way. His life after he made the decision to trust God and give up his fast-track way of living was and is significantly different from his life before that decision.

Upturn or Downturn

In business, we are accustomed to seeing graphs that record sales. In life, performance might be charted in a similar fashion. For example, in dealing with the family domain, we may see a downturn when a job becomes all-consuming and the family is neglected, or even a very serious downturn if someone experiences a divorce or a serious estrangement from a child. In like manner, we may see an upturn in an act of reconciliation.

A turning point is invariably toward or away from the best of God's LifePlan for you. It is a point in which things move toward a greater good or toward a worse state. The point actually may be a phase or a period of time, but it is always a mark of transition to a new state. It is significant because it is a marker of change.

Toward or Away from God

For committed believers, a turning point invariably is a change of some type that brings us closer to God or farther away from Him. We are always in a constant dynamic of drawing closer to our Creator and His intended purpose for us and relationship with us, or we are moving away from our Creator and His plan and purpose.

We may not be consciously aware that we are making this decision, but we make a decision nonetheless. Some of us will say, "I started doing my own thing . . . ," or "I started going back to church. . . ." The point may not be an open act of rebellion or of recommitment to Christ Jesus, but it functions in our life history as a point that alters the course of the spiritual life.

Because turning points draw us toward God or move us away from Him, they draw us toward something that is God-approved, or "good," or they move us toward something that is God-disapproved, or "bad." A person who becomes converted or makes a full surrender late in life can usually chart the turning points fairly readily because she has lived to see the outcome of the decision: "I shouldn't have married that person," "I made a mistake in choosing that career path," or "I should have started going to church sooner than I did."

These are statements I have heard a number of times. They are not statements that seem directly related to a person's faith relationship with God, and yet they reflect a turning point that moved that person closer to God and the doing of His will in his life, or farther away from God and toward the pursuit of his own pleasure and purpose.

All Turning Points Are Significant

In my early years of facilitating LifePlans for people, I attempted to help them prioritize their turning points, isolating which turning points were the most significant or which had the greatest impact.

I no longer do that. I realized after talking to dozens of people that *all* turning points are significant because they are points of life change.

Not All Changes Are Turning Points

Not all changes are turning points. A person may move to a new city, enter a different church, receive a promotion—all of which may involve life stress, but none of which may indicate a life change, especially if the person attends a church of the same denomination and continues to work in the same general area for the same company. In this example, a person is continuing in the same direction with greater intensity or a greater breadth of experience. Nothing significant has changed about the person's relationship with God. A genuine change of career, however, is likely to be a turning point.

One woman who came for a LifePlan facilitation initially marked the birth of each of her children as a turning point. However, this family path was a continuous one in direction. No true turning point emerged.

In contrast, the birth of a child with a disability in one client's family was a significant turning point since much about the family's routine, the vocation of the parent, and the parent's involvement with the church took a dramatic turn.

Don't struggle to force something to be a turning point that isn't one. Generally speaking, if you put something of minor importance on the list, you'll likely discover that you struggle when you attempt to describe it in terms of meaning. If you discover that something is not a turning point, eliminate it.

Just remember that a turning point is *not* a continuation of the status quo of your life.

Universal Turning Points

Conversion and surrender experiences are always major turning points in a person's life. Life after a genuine spiritual conversion is not the same as life before conversion. Life after a complete surrender to Christ's will is not the same as life before that surrender moment.

By comparison, the joining of a church may not be a major turning point if nothing of a spiritual nature has taken place as part of that event.

Marriage is always a turning point, and so is divorce or the death of a spouse. In each case, life after these events is not the same as life before them.

How Many Turning Points?

It is not unusual for a person who is fifty to have fifteen or twenty turning points. Some people have fewer. A few have more.

THE STEPS FOR DOING A TURNING POINTS PROFILE

There are four main steps in doing a Turning Points Profile. We will cover only the first two in this chapter.

STEP #1: IDENTIFY ALL TRUE TURNING POINTS

Let your mind wander freely over the course of your personal history to pinpoint and list the events that you believe to be the most significant ones in your life. Don't force yourself to maintain an age-sequence orderly process at the outset of listing the turning points. Creating a composite list is the starting point. A sequence over time can be plotted easily once the list is complete.

Be sure to identify each turning point. If you miss one, you've missed something important.

Give yourself sufficient time for this process. This is not a process that can or should be hurried if it is to have significant meaning to you and be used by the Holy Spirit. God is never in a hurry. He desires to reveal certain things to you, but you very well may need to be in a state of inner calm before you will hear what the Spirit has to say.

Certain events or changes may come to mind as you reflect on the key periods in your life. When I facilitate a LifePlan for a person, the turning points process usually takes an entire day, generally an eight-hour session. In all likelihood, you will need to spend at least eight hours in this process if you are attempting to list your turning points on your own, especially since you will not have the benefit of a facilitator to help you probe your past. Unless you have gone on a personal retreat solely for the purpose of engaging in the LifePlanning process, you will probably need to spend several shorter sessions identifying your turning points.

Recognize that minor events can have major consequences. In my experience of facilitating LifePlans, I find that about 20 percent of the turning points that a person lists are subtle ones. I refer to them as "Behold!" moments. They are relationships or situations that we generally do not think of as being highly significant, but upon reflection, we discover their true meaning in our lives and we feel like saying, "Behold, the hand of God at work!"

My personal example. To help you see how a Turning Points Profile might be constructed, I am going to share with you some of my life story.

When I was twelve years old, I presented myself to be baptized at the altar of the Methodist church in my local community. Ours was not a churchgoing family. I had good parents, but they didn't attend church at any point during my childhood. Why did I take this step on my own at the age of twelve? I believe it was a God-driven experience. I took this initiative without any encouragement or support from family or friends. I got up one Sunday morning and went to church on my own and went to the altar at the appropriate time in the service and joined the church. I began to attend regularly from that point.

That was the first spiritual turning point in my life. It was my introduction to the things of God and to involvement with a church community. It was my initiation into the faith kingdom of God.

A major turning point occurred in my life the night I went to a high school dance, walked across the floor as the record player began to play a Glenn Miller tune, and asked a girl named Ginny White to dance with me. I had never had a date before that night. As we danced, I fell in love with Ginny. More than fifty years later, I can still describe for you the way she looked that night—her skating skirt lined with red satin, her black sweater, the white pearls she wore. My life after that first dance was not the same as my life before that moment.

I certainly had a lot to learn about love. After all, I was only fifteen the night I met Ginny. My love for my wife today is far greater than the love of that first night. Nevertheless, the turning point occurred at the moment I met Ginny. My life took a decided turn. Everything after that was an ongoing process in my relationship with my sweetheart.

The period of my courtship with Ginny—from age fifteen to age nineteen—began with a turning point, a dance. It ended with a turning point, our wedding. At the time of my marriage, I also entered college and began to work full-time.

The years immediately after our marriage were important—in some ways difficult, in other ways blissful. We lived in a twenty-three-dollar-a-month, cold-water flat, four flights up—making our home in a ghetto area, singing in bed as we ate saltine crackers and apples, harmonizing our lives as one. Our son Tom Jr. was born, and he was two years old by the time I graduated. They were wonderful foundation-laying years, but in and of themselves, they didn't have any major turning point. As a whole, they were a continuation of the turning point that might be described "Marry/Start Family and Career."

I did experience a turning point the night our daughter, Debbie, was born. We had three sons by the time she arrived. I had always wanted a daughter, and the night she was born was a night of pure ecstasy for me. It was a transcendent night for me. It is the only time I have ever felt as if I were floating in joy. I felt I had a glimpse of heaven. I went to a nearby diner after her birth, which was late at night, and I bought the meal of everybody who was there. I had to do *something* to express part of the feelings I had inside me. That night for me was a turning point; my life was not to be the same. I had an overwhelming feeling of thanksgiving and gratitude to God.

The day my little girl died of spinal cancer, at age twelve, was also a turning point. As ecstatic as I had been at her birth, I was just that devastated at her death. I entered a period of insufferable grief. I hit the bottom of my life.

I began to attempt to drown my sorrow and grief in alcohol. It was not a conscious decision, of course, but neither was it an excuse. It was also something that I realized then and now as a failed method. The alcohol never fully numbed my intense pain and grief. Eventually I was drinking half to three-quarters of a bottle of whiskey a night.

I truly believe that I would not have lived very many years had I not made a change in my behavior. There's a Chinese saying: "Man takes a drink. The drink takes a drink. Drink takes the man." When "drink takes a drink," the drinking is symptomatic. A person drinks out of habit, not desire. The addiction has not fully taken hold at this point, but the person is on the verge of being addicted to alcohol. That's the point at which I found myself.

I finally reached the point where I threw my hands in the air and said, "God, take over. I can't handle this." I was instantly cured of my reliance on alcohol. I relied instead on the Lord. I have never been drunk since that moment thirty years ago. I have no need to turn to alcohol for relief of any inner pain, sorrow, or trouble I experience.

I wanted the Lord to help me with other issues. I was seeking peace from the grief, the root cause of my drinking. The title of Fulton Sheen's classic best-seller in the 1940s, *Peace of Soul,* describes exactly what I most needed and desired. When I turned my life over to God, I received that peace. That was my point of conversion, of accepting Jesus as my Savior and Lord. It was a significant turning point in my life.

Another turning point was related to Debbie's death, but it involved my wife, Ginny. After Debbie died, Ginny became suicidal. I didn't know that with certainty until just a few years ago when she admitted to me that she had been suicidal, but I knew in my heart at the time that in her grief, Ginny longed to be with Debbie in death more than she desired to be with me and our sons in life. She had stopped eating and was down to eighty-five pounds. She had little interest in me or in our life as a family.

I recently learned that 85 percent of all marriages end in divorce after the death of a child. That may have been true for us, but the greater likelihood was that our marriage would have ended in my wife's death.

At the time Debbie died, we had one son still living at home—he was fourteen. Our older two sons had left home to enter college. Within a period of six months, Ginny had gone from being the mother of four active children at home to being the mother of one son at home. The loss was more than she could bear.

When I gave my life to Christ, God began to speak to me. He gave me His plan for achieving full recovery and for turning what the enemy had meant for evil to a great good. He spoke in my spirit, *Adopt.* My boss at the RCA Corporation was Ted Smith, executive vice president and television pioneer. He said, "Come back east with me, Tom." We went back to our roots, for Ginny and I had been raised on the East Coast. That dear, gentle man got me through the hardest years of my life. Had he ever raised his voice, I would have shattered. God put me with Ted, of that I have no doubt.

After Ginny and I returned to our roots, we actively pursued adoption. We were turned down repeatedly. The reason generally given was that bereaved, grieving parents do not make good adoptive parents. Even so, each time we were turned down we said, "We still want to adopt." I knew in my heart that adoption was the right thing for us.

Then one day the Children's Aid Society of Philadelphia called and said, "Are you still interested in adopting?" I said, "Yes."

The person from the society replied, "You haven't taken no for an answer. Our question for you now is, Will you take *three* children?" I didn't even hesitate. I said, "You bet." The three children were from the same family initially. They had been separated and placed into two foster homes. They were reunited as siblings when we adopted them.

With the adoption of those three children, I got back my wife, my best friend, my lover. Our sons got their mother back. My wife got her life back. Adoption was a turning point.

The experience was also a turning point in another dimension outside my vocation and my family life. God had said to me, *Go home,* and I obeyed. He had said to me, *Adopt,* and I obeyed. That was a spiritual milestone for me in my move toward God and toward the pursuit of God's will. I had learned to hear and obey.

As Ginny became truly alive again, a functioning mother and wife, I sensed that she wished to return to California. I called her into the living room of our home in Valley Forge one evening and said simply, "We are going back to California."

She replied just as simply, "We don't have to."

I said, "Yes, we do."

We went around that loop three or four times, and then she said, "How soon can we go?" Once again, God had nudged me in the right direction.

Ginny asked, "What will you do there?"

I said, "I don't have the faintest idea. I just know that I need to take you home."

She said, "Well, if it doesn't work out, will you lay the blame at my feet?"

I said, "Never. We are a team. We will make it through this. Where I work is my business; where we live is *our* business."

We moved. I made a life-changing decision to become a consultant. I had never anticipated that I would choose to earn a living as a consultant. Frankly I hadn't liked most of the consultants with whom I had been forced to work in my corporate positions. I found them overbearing and arrogant, giving unworkable advice and then leaving people to struggle under the burden of their plans. I certainly didn't want to be a know-it-all consultant. That change in vocation was a turning point.

The next real turning point of my life came when I realized that I was not the person that I wanted to be. For several years after Debbie's death, I threw myself into my work. I did virtually nothing for myself. I spent little time with my family. I was not growing as a person. I made a conscious, serious decision that I was going to change my ways. I heard about an executive management course at Pepperdine University. In my interview for the program, Dr. Wayne Strom, head of the Behavioral Faculty at the time, asked me just one question, "Why do you want to take the course?"

I replied, "I want to begin growing again."

He said, "You're in."

I started the program, and I grew. I was voted by my colleagues in that program as the "most changed" student who took the degree plan. I know today that I could not teach the group sessions in my strategic planning consulting, nor could I have developed the Life-Plan process, without that training.

The course at Pepperdine University was at least 60 percent behavioral in nature. When I had gone to college, psychology was largely limited to Freud and Jung. Suddenly I was exposed to Carl Rogers and all of the other modern behavioral psychologists. I began to see how my reactions to Ginny and my family were rooted in my past.

I am the product of a fairly militaristic father. He was the best father he knew how to be. I know that he loved me. But I didn't receive praise, affirmation, or appreciation from him, much less unconditional love. My father had a profound influence on my life. I spent decades looking for the love he could not give me. In retrospect I can see why God put Ginny in my life when I was just in my early teens.

I thought I had to work two or three times harder and longer than any other person to be worth anything. What I achieved at work gave me value. And yet, it never seemed to be enough. Along the way, of course, I did good work. I had a part in creating products that people routinely use today. I'm proud of my work record and level of achievement. But my motivation was wrong, and inside, despite the achievements, I wasn't happy.

The course at Pepperdine gave me many insights about *why* I had become the unhappy man I was.

Out of that realization grew an intense desire to have a different type of relationship with my wife and children from what I had experienced in the past. My relationship with my wife had deteriorated; I had strong suspicions she was on the brink of divorcing me. I didn't have a good relationship with my children.

I had a very quick temper and was very impatient prior to taking that course. I recall one time twenty-eight years earlier when our son Tom was young. I became totally exasperated with him at the dinner table and snapped, "You're acting just like a two-year-old."

Ginny asked me very calmly, "Tom, how old is he?" I was caught short. My son *was* two years old.

A short-fused, work-driven man! I wasn't who I wanted to be, and I was miserable. In more than thirty years of marriage, I had not become the man, the husband, or the father I wanted to be.

The behavioral insights I gained week by week in that course helped me to achieve the change I desired. One of the most important assignments in the program was to write our own epitaphs. I struggled with preparing the statement about how I would want to be remembered after my death. I wanted to be a genuine friend to my children when they became adults. I wanted to be remembered by my wife as an extremely loving and kind husband. When I read what I had written, I came to the stark realization that I wasn't the man I had described. I had a great deal of changing and growing to do if I was to be that man by the time I died. *I chose to change.*

Ten years after that exercise, I came across the epitaph I had written, and I said to Ginny, "Here, I want you to read this."

"What is it?" she asked.

"My epitaph," I said.

"That's pretty morbid," she responded.

"No, I don't think so," I said. "It's something I wrote a decade ago. I want you to tell me very honestly if this is the way you will remember me. This is the kind of man I want to be in your memory and the memory of our children."

She read through what I had written and then said, "Yes, Tom, that's the man you are. That's the way the children and I think of you now."

That was one of the best moments of my life because I knew that I had achieved something that I had set out ten years before to achieve. I am a very different person today. The course at Pepperdine was a significant turning point in my life.

There were several major turning points in my life between the time of my marriage to Ginny and the day I made a decision that I was going to redefine myself as a man, a husband, and a father. Those turning points were largely vocational.

In the aftermath of Debbie's death, my wife went back to nursing. She totally redid her academic and nursing training and then dedicated all of her nursing effort to Debbie's memory. She believed that Debbie would have been a nurse, so she practiced for ten years, until 1988, in her honor. In the course of the years that Ginny was a nurse, she had an opportunity to impact hundreds upon hundreds of lives; she truly was one of the greatest nurses that God ever created. She once told me that she loved caring for patients so much that it didn't seem right to take money for her service.

One of the main turning points after I redefined myself as a man, a husband, and a father was the death of our son Tom Jr. when he was only thirty-seven years old.

My son died while on a fishing trip to Alaska. His amphibious plane took off in gusty winds. The plane's wing dipped into the waters, and the plane cartwheeled and broke up on impact. Tom and several others managed to crawl out onto a pontoon after the crash, but Tom went back into the plane in an attempt to help a man who couldn't swim. They made it back out onto the pontoon, but then the pontoon broke up. Tom was wearing waders, and when he entered the lake, they immediately filled with water and he drowned. Only one of the men survived.

My son Tom died calling to the heavens, "Dear Jesus, I love You!" We sing a hymn that says, "With my dying breath I will confess my love to You." That hymn was a reality in my son's life.

Shortly before takeoff, the wealthy philanthropist who was sitting in the copilot's seat of that plane had said to those aboard, "This is the day that the Lord has made. We will accept what it brings." Only minutes later, he and my son were in heaven.

Shortly after Debbie died, Tom Jr. attended a Billy Graham Crusade at the Los Angeles Coliseum. He went down on the field to accept Christ and give his life to Him. He gave up a very promising art career as a painter to become a minister.

As an associate pastor, Tom was forced to leave three churches. In all three cases, the senior pastors had a young dynamic earth-moving entrepreneur at their side, but I believe they didn't know how to handle him. To each of them, Tom was a "control problem." They didn't know what they had. Had any of those good pastors challenged Tom with building something from scratch, he would have been overjoyed with the results.

For his part, Tom Jr. didn't know who he was. He saw his failures and felt they must reflect a problem resident in himself. He came to me in tears. I did a LifePlan consultation for him, and the result was that my son formed Tom Paterson Jr. Ministries, with a focus on raising funds for Christian schools. In what were to be the last two years of his life, Tom knew his greatest success. He was doing what God had gifted him to do, and he felt freely released to do it.

Tom Jr. lived a victorious life. He died a victorious death. After Tom died, my life changed. I began to live my life to *serve* others as I never had before. Prior to that time, I worked to provide for my family and to achieve as much as possible in my career. After Tom's death, I saw work in terms of helping others. As Ginny had gone back to nursing in Debbie's honor, I began to think in terms of doing something in honor of Tom Jr. At that time, I readily admit, the nudging in that direction was gentle, the slightest of movements—it was real and significant nonetheless.

Even with a renewed interest in helping others, from the time of my conversion until just a few years ago, I was a casual Christian. If you had asked me, "Were you a Christian?" I certainly would have said I was—and indeed, I believe I was. I had accepted Christ Jesus as my Savior and had received by faith God's gift of forgiveness and eternal life. I came to a point of full surrender, however, in which I said to God, "Take all of me. All that I am, all that I have, all that I do, all that I will become. I want all of Christ and I want all of me to belong to Christ." My surrender to God was a significant turning point—a time after which my life was no longer the same. My life became completely Christ-centered as the result of that experience.

A summary. Now, given what I have told you, I feel certain that you would be able to identify a number of turning points in my life. A list might include these turning points:

1. Baptized
2. Met Ginny
3. Married Ginny/started college/began work

4. Debbie's birth
5. Debbie's death
6. Conversion to Christ
7. Began consulting
8. Adopted three children
9. Redefined self
10. Tom's death
11. Surrendered

Label the Turning Points

As you identify each turning point, give it a name or brief description. This will be the headline for your turning point. Limit your label to one or two words as I did. Then give a brief statement of meaning that may be related to that headline.

For example, in my description of Debbie's death, I might have used these words:

> *Debbie's death*
> Hit bottom, intense
> grief, became a
> miserable drinker

In describing my conversion experience, I might have said:

> *Conversion*
> "Couldn't handle it"; God
> gave peace, freedom
> from alcohol

Be concise, but be meaningful in your descriptions.

As you may have already concluded, one of my heroes is Winston Churchill. I credit him, along with his friend Franklin Roosevelt, with saving Western civilization. One of the hallmarks of Churchill's life was that he had a way with words. He was an expert at crafting the quotable quote.

Behind quotable quotes, however, are well-crafted thoughts. Thoughtsmithing is crafting a thought to the point that it catches the truth in very few words. Distilled thought is very close to the essence of a matter; it is true substance in the invisible realm.

For example, Churchill once said, "Everyone wants to learn but no one wants to be taught." There's a world of truth in that one sentence. No one wants to be lectured or preached to, but all of us take joy in learning.

I once told my son Tom Jr. that the human attention span is long enough to accommodate ten compliments, five judgments, or one preachment. He didn't particularly want to hear that since he was a preacher, but I stand by my estimate. He argued, "But I'm a preacher." I replied, "Don't preach!"

As you are evaluating and labeling the turning points of your life, choose to become a thoughtsmith. Capture the essence of that period or event in your life in as few and as provocative words as possible.

STEP #2: CONSTRUCT A TURNING POINTS MATRIX

Place your turning points into sequence on a time line. In the matrix, this time line is labeled "Age" and "Events."

Put your age (or age range) above the line.

Put your turning points from left to right in the "Personal" column below the line since all turning points are related to the personal Life Domain. A turning point isn't a turning point if it doesn't impact your personal domain. As you move through the Life Domains, describe not only what happened but also why the event was meaningful.

Add as Necessary

As you place events on this matrix, feel free to add turning points you may not have considered previously. All turning points must be included for the matrix to yield meaningful truth.

Then indicate which Life Domains other than the personal domain were impacted by the turning point event or period. Don't stretch or force an extension to other domains, however.

Certainly all major events impact the whole of your life, but in most cases, a turning point event or period is concentrated in one or two Life Domains. For example, "Age 22—Got Married" will likely impact the personal and family domains. It will impact only marginally vocation, church/faith kingdom, and community domains, but to apply it to these domains is a stretch. The event should probably be limited to only two domains.

Once you have identified all the domains in which the turning point should be placed, briefly describe the way in which the turning point impacted the Life Domain. For example, "Age 13—Joined Boy Scouts" might be the general label, and the description might be, "Took me off the streets, out of a gang." In applying this to other domains, one might place it under the church/faith kingdom domain if the Scout troop was affiliated with a church. Under this domain, the description might be, "Began to attend church, made friends at church." The event might have impacted the community domain since the boy's relationship with his neighborhood friends might have changed. He might write under community, "Old friends retaliated, then ignored me."

These descriptions provide in cursory fashion a sense of meaning for each turning point period or event. They go beyond *what* occurred to hint at the *impact* the turning point had on the person's future. Just as in the initial description of the event, be concise.

Here is a sample to show how turning points might be charted across Life Domains.

SAMPLE

TURNING POINTS MATRIX

LIFE DOMAINS	AGE: 8–12 EVENTS:	13	14
PERSONAL	"Home School" Great intellectual growth but a growing sense of social isolation	"Church Choir" Become active member of church choir, friends galore recognize singing talent	"Conversion" Accept Jesus as personal Savior and Lord
FAMILY	One sibling stays at home for home school; another goes to public school; sibling rift begins		Able to forgive problem sibling
CHURCH/ FAITH KINGDOM		Through attending church choir, introduced to gospel	Feel full acceptance at church, active in membership
VOCATION			Begin to take music lessions; compete in local music competition; give music lessons to neighbor child
COMMUNITY			Join community wide church youth choir

Now, complete your Turning Points Matrix on the form provided. Again, give yourself sufficient time for this process. Reflect deeply. Ask the Holy Spirit to bring to your mind *all* of the events that have been turning points.

YOUR TURNING POINTS MATRIX

LIFE DOMAINS	EVENTS:
PERSONAL	
FAMILY	
CHURCH/ FAITH KINGDOM	
VOCATION	
COMMUNITY	

7

THE TURNING POINTS PROFILE

Part 2
Drawing Meaning from Your Matrix

Where we find ourselves today—closer to God or more remote, on or off the track vocationally or in our family or personal lives—can be seen clearly through the perspective of our turning points and their control path.

A Turning Points Matrix yields significant information for you, but there are two ways of approaching a matrix that allow you to gain even more meaning from it. Meaning ultimately brings you to greater perspective and to the truth of your LifePlan. The two additional steps in this chapter build upon those in the previous chapter.

STEP #3: IDENTIFY THE CONTROL PATH

To identify the control path, use a colored pencil or highlighter to mark the Life Domains that have been impacted during a turning point. Then connect the shaded areas.

The resulting flow of color across the history of your life is what I term the *control path.* It reveals the focus of your time and energy. You can see this pattern without the shading, but most people gain new insight with this technique.

Given the sample matrix from the previous chapter, in slightly abbreviated form, let me show you how such a control path might appear using light pencil shading rather than color.

SAMPLE
TURNING POINTS MATRIX WITH CONTROL PATH IDENTIFIED

LIFE DOMAINS	AGE: 8–12 EVENTS:	13	14
PERSONAL	"Home School" Great intellectual growth but a growing sense of social isolation	"Church Choir" Become active member of church choir, friends galore recognize singing talent	"Conversion" Accept Jesus as personal Savior and Lord
FAMILY	One sibling stays at home for home school; another goes to public school; sibling rift begins		Able to forgive problem sibling
CHURCH/ FAITH KINGDOM		Through attending church choir, introduced to gospel	Feel full acceptance at church, active in membership
VOCATION			Begin to take music lessions; compete in local music competition; give music lessons to neighbor child
COMMUNITY			Join community wide church youth choir

Return to the previous chapter, and highlight your control path at this point. Reflect on what you see there. Look for patterns and meaning in your control path.

Highlighting the control path gives a perspective about the balance of your life as well as the general results that key decisions and events seem to cause. If you see, for example, that nearly all of your energy seems to be focused on vocation, you may very well conclude that vocation has been the dominant theme of your life, likely to the neglect of other areas.

You will also see the focus of energy during any one period. In our sample, the person's early years were limited to personal and family domains, which is likely to be the case for most people.

In some cases, people have been able to look at a control path and conclude, "After that point, things went downhill." The converse is also true. Others have looked at a control path and con cluded about a turning point, "That was the best decision I ever made because after that things really took an upswing."

Briefly describe the meaning you see in your control path:

MEANING I SEE IN MY CONTROL PATH

____

____

____

____

____

____

____

____

____

____

____

____

____

____

____

STEP #4: IDENTIFY LIFE GATES

A Life Gate might be considered a supra-turning point. It is a supreme event. Generally, all domains of life are impacted in a powerful way. In looking for Life Gates, you are looking for points at which major doors were opened wide or slammed shut.

The Apostle Paul as an Example

In my study of the life of the apostle Paul, I realized that what happened to Saul of Tarsus (Paul) on the road to Damascus was a Life Gate experience. His encounter with the risen Christ changed his life in all ways, and it also changed the course of Christianity. The slayer of Christians became the most ardent soul winner.

As a result of what happened to Paul in that encounter with Christ, his personal and church/faith kingdom domains were dramatically changed, and his family life no doubt changed significantly. We know very little of Paul's relationship with a wife or children, but we do know that he moved away from the religious community in which he had been a leader, and he subsequently spent more than a decade in an isolated environment in which the Lord taught him directly and privately. Such a change had to impact his family domain.

In like manner, Paul's vocation changed. He may have been a leather craftsman both before and after his conversion, a vocation often translated as "tent maker" in the Scriptures. But the place of vocation changed in his life. It became a secondary means to serving Christ and ministering to others. It was a means to an end—the preaching of the gospel in various Gentile cities—rather than an end that justified all other means.

Paul's community changed. No longer was he identified among the zealous, religious community of Jews in Jerusalem, but he was identified among the Christians, especially those in Damascus, and increasingly so among the Gentile Christian community in cities such as Ephesus, Athens, and other cities in Greece and Asia Minor.

In sum, Paul's old life was not Paul's new life in any way.

Such a change signifies that God has closed a door—definitively and completely—upon one's past life and simultaneously opened a door—widely and obviously—upon a new life.

This is a passage that I term a *Life Gate.* A person has moved through a transition period or event that changes all of life significantly. Once a person goes through that gate, there's no turning back. It's as if the gate closes behind the person, completely shutting off a return to the past.

Because you have free will, you can attempt to move back to a previous position. In reality, however, you are on the hook, and God is reeling you into His new plan for you. He may allow you plenty of line to swim as far and as fast as possible. He may allow you to put up a real fight, struggling against the hook that has caught you. But you have entered a new dimension of God's plan for you.

In the end, you of your own volition submit or yield. Saul was one of God's elect, predestined to become Paul. He was free to struggle, he had, as all of us do, a free will, and he would freely submit. Paul had done his best to persecute the early Christians. He had no intention of becoming a Christian; the very idea was totally alien and even loathsome to him. His encounter with the risen Christ on the road to Damascus was an experience, however, from which he could not escape. He had options, but only one that was viable: to yield to Christ and to follow Him as Savior and Lord.

All Things Are Made New

With a Life Gate, God closes off your old life, opens the gate to a new life, or does both simultaneously. *All* things in your life are made new in the process (Rom. 6:4).

Genuine conversion to Christ is a Life Gate experience, and so is total surrender. I contend that a person has not truly been converted to Christ or made a complete surrender of life if all of life's domains have not been impacted.

We must be cautious in assuming that all personal conversion experiences are true Life Gates. Merely joining a church, making a public confession of faith, or coming to a point of believing in Jesus as Savior may or may not be a Life Gate experience, depending on the meaning that the person had for the experience and the impact of the experience on the person's future.

Of course, other events apart from spiritual commitment to the Lord qualify as Life Gates.

A man came to me after his company had been acquired by a new corporation and he had been told that his services would no longer be needed. He wanted me to help him determine the direction his future should take. He needed precise guidance.

He came to a number of life-changing decisions in the course of discovering his LifePlan. He saw with new insight his real giftedness. He realized that he needed to move to a different part of the country, an area where he had family ties that were important to him and to his wife. He identified the type of position that was most appropriate for him to pursue, as well as the type of company for which he wanted to work. Most important, he completely surrendered his life to Christ Jesus.

From the time he sat in my home office, coming to a new awareness of God's plan and purpose for his life and making a decision to pursue God's plan and not his own, his life took on a completely different nature. Nothing of the old was brought forward into the new except his relationship with his wife. There is very little comparison between the way he was living prior to this decision and the way he is living now. He found a new job, one completely in keeping with his giftedness and his heart's desires. His family life was renewed. His personal life was enriched in ways it had never been before. He entered a deeper and fulfilling relationship with Christ Jesus. His community changed. For him, the LifePlan process itself became a Life Gate!

Life Gates in Mother Teresa's Life

At age twelve Agnes Gonxha Bojaxhiu, later to be known as Mother Teresa, told her mother that she wished to join the church. At eighteen she went from Albania to Ireland, joining the Sisters of Loreto. She knew then that her vocation would be to help the poor. At nineteen God called her to India, where she taught for almost two decades. That is not the Mother Teresa the world knows or reveres today. Nevertheless, those years as a teacher were a part of God's growing and maturing process, strengthening her faith for her God-given mission. His master thought for the young nun was for her to become Mother Teresa.

Then, while she was on a train to Darjeeling, a mountain resort in northeast India, the Lord called her to undertake the mission of serving the unloved, unwanted, destitute, and dying. This was a call within a call. Later she explained, "The message was quite clear. It was an order. I was to leave the convent. God wanted something more from me. He wanted me to be poor and to love Him in the distressing disguise of the poorest of the poor."[1] Everything about her life changed.

Mother Teresa began her work among the poorest of the poor—people dying on the streets in Calcutta. Today, more than four hundred homes of her order, the Missionaries of Charity, can be found in more than 120 nations.

Two Life Gate experiences were likely involved. The first was her calling to be a nun and to work as a missionary. That experience gave her a focus that changed everything in her life. Her past and future were not the same. The second was on the train to Darjeeling when she knew with certainty that the time had come for her to engage in the work that was God's master thought for her. That turning point in her life impacted all future decisions; it was a point of no return for her.

A Life Gate Experience in My Life

Apart from my conversion and surrender experiences, the time in which we moved and adopted children was a Life Gate experience for me, as well as for Ginny. That decision impacted me on the personal level—my personal routine and concerns changed. It obviously impacted me in the family domain—I again became the father of three young children. It impacted my vocation since I moved into a new phase of my career—consulting—and my community dramatically in moving to a new location. The decision also impacted me spiritually because it was one of the first times that I knowingly felt that God had spoken to me directly and personally His plan and His direction. I was aware that I could hear His voice in my spirit.

How Many Life Gates?

Generally speaking, most people have very few Life Gates, perhaps only three or four.

Paul obviously had a Life Gate experience on the Damascus Road. His call to the Greek world, which many refer to as his Macedonian call, may have been another. His arrest in Jerusalem, which eventually led to his martyrdom in Rome, may have been yet another. In each case, all of life's domains were impacted, and each marked the passing through a door that was shut behind Paul as soon as he passed through it. In each case, once Paul had experienced the turning point, he was not able to return fully to any aspect of his former life.

PART OF GOD'S PLAN FOR ALL

A Life Gate is an integral part of God's plan for each of His elect children.

Very often, a Life Gate event is marked by a direct experience with God—perhaps hearing the voice of God, having a vision from God, gaining a strong insight from God. Experiencing a Life Gate is a God-moment; tears of joy and wonder are likely to flow as we are struck by the majesty of God's orchestration of our lives. In all cases, the Holy Spirit is at work to reveal a Life Gate to us. The apostle Paul wrote,

> **"Eye has not seen, nor ear heard,**
> **Nor have entered into the heart of man**
> **The things which God has prepared for those who love Him."**
> **But God has revealed them to us through His Spirit. For the Spirit searches all things, yes, the deep things of God.** (1 Cor. 2:9–10)

The Holy Spirit is both the agent of Life Gate experiences and the revealer of them to our conscious understanding.

All Turning Points Must Be Present

It is impossible to discern a Life Gate unless all of the relevant turning points have been identified and developed.

All Turning Points Must Be Applied Properly to Life Domains

To discern a Life Gate quickly, apply all turning points properly and completely to the Life Domains.

In some cases, the community domain is the one area that may not appear readily to be impacted by a genuine Life Gate experience. Upon probing, however, I usually find that the domain was impacted, although perhaps more subtly. One's friends may change. One's associations and affiliations may change. One may not move physically, but within a location, one's identity may take on a different definition.

In a genuine Life Gate, all domains are impacted without stretching the event to force it to have more meaning than it has. Nevertheless, do not neglect to explore the possibility that additional Life Domains may have been impacted by what you consider to be major milestones.

OPENING OR CLOSING?

A Life Gate marks the ending of a time of preparation or service (a closing) or signals that an incredible mission is about to begin (an opening).

Most people have no difficulty in discerning whether a Life Gate is an opening or a closing, or both. A man once labeled a period in his life as "Hit Bottom—Age 36." In all ways, his life seemed to fall apart at that point. The events impacted his family, his vocation, his relationship with the church and with God, and his involvement with his community. The Life Gate was clearly a closing of his old life.

In his case, and in the case of some LifePlan clients, an opening was to be found directly on the other side of the closing. In many cases, however, a period of preparation follows a closing. Various things may be required before an opening Life Gate experience occurs. But you can know with certainty that when God closes the door on an old life, He *will* open a new one at the point that you are ready to move through it.

Beginning Point, Not Arrival Point

A Life Gate experience does not mean that you have arrived fully at your potential or purpose in life. Once you are past the Life Gate event or decision, growth continues. The apostle Paul had a growing period ahead of him after he bowed his knee to Christ.

The value of recognizing Life Gates is that you might see the next stage of development, training, building, and maturing that is required of you. You are drawn closer to God as you acknowledge His hand at work.

SAMPLE
TURNING POINTS MATRIX WITH LIFE GATE IDENTIFIED AND LABELED

LIFE DOMAINS	AGE: 8–12 EVENTS:	13	14
PERSONAL	"Home School"	"Church Choir"	"Conversion"
FAMILY			Able to forgive problem sibling
CHURCH/ FAITH KINGDOM		Introduced to gospel through church choir	Active in church
VOCATION			Begin to take, give music lessions; compete locally
COMMUNITY			Join community youth choir

LIFE GATE
Future in church music is established

MARK AND LABEL YOUR LIFE GATES

Here the Life Gate is clearly identified for the previous example:

You will note in the example that all Life Domains are involved. You no doubt can anticipate how significant this Life Gate was to this person's subsequent turning points.

Now refer to your Turning Points Matrix in the previous chapter. Identify *your* Life Gates.

Then give each of your Life Gates a label and a brief descriptor of meaning as you perceive it. I added such a label and descriptor to our previous example.

Take a few moments after you have identified and labeled your Life Gates to reflect on them. A variety of meanings and emotions are likely to fill your being. Allow the Holy Spirit to do His work.

I suggest that at this point in the process you take time to rest. A thorough evaluation of your turning points is a strenuous, long process. It can be emotionally draining. Give yourself a break before you return, with perhaps renewed energy and fresh insights, to the final stage of the process. Revisit your Turning Points Profile with fresh eyes.

GLEANING NEW INSIGHTS FROM YOUR TURNING POINTS PROFILE

The net result of this one activity in the LifePlanning process is generally a new awareness that God has been present in your life all along—and what's more, He has been *active* (Deut. 33:27).

An Awareness of God's Active Presence

You have times when you feel more keenly the presence of God. You may say, "God is far away," or "God is very close to me." The reality is that God never moves from you. He is always very present and available to you. What happens is that you, through decisions and behaviors, are more aware or less aware of God at work in you. Sinful behavior and a callous attitude toward God are walls that *you* erect between yourself and your loving, forgiving heavenly Father.

God is not inaccessible to you; rather, you make yourself inaccessible to Him. You create a gulf that separates you from openly receiving all that He freely offers.

Stated another way, whenever you separate yourself from God, you have entered a faith shutdown. All that you receive from God—be it salvation, the gift of the Holy Spirit, emotional or physical healing, daily guidance, any of His gifts—you receive by faith. When you deactivate your faith in God, you put yourself into a position where you are not open to receiving fully all that God desires for you to receive. Willful rebellion and active faith cannot coexist. When you rebel against God and His love, His commandments, and His presence, you shut down your faith. When you choose to obey and trust God, you activate your faith.

The turning points process, including the identification of Life Gates, usually reveals key points in life during which you actively, and by the exercise of will and faith, moved *dramatically* toward God or away from God—perhaps stated more accurately, these are times or events in which you tore down the walls of separation between yourself and God, or built up walls of separation.

Equally true, an analysis of turning points and Life Gates usually reveals that God has been present all along, always holding out a Plan B as a means of reentering the stream of the fullness of His LifePlan. God always provides a means for you to regain a full, active, and completely surrendered relationship with Him. He always holds out to you His unconditional love, forgiveness, and outpouring of His presence and power in your life.

You can't help seeing God's hand very clearly when you look at your history. Especially by the time you reach middle age, you generally have a number of times to which you can point and say, "If God hadn't brought me through that, I wouldn't be here today."

By the time we are in our forties and fifties, most of us recognize that we are not capable of engineering miracles, blessings, or obvious sovereign gifts and acts of God. We recognize instead that we tend to be very capable of engineering our mistakes and failures.

Time and again people say to me with humility and awe, "God was there all along, wasn't He, Tom?" This awareness of God's ongoing presence and work in their lives is a powerful prerequisite to an awareness of the other gifts and abilities that God has built into their nature.

When people see God at work in their personal histories, they are much quicker to identify God at work in the creation of their giftedness and spiritual DNA.

Often, the recognition of Life Gates humbles and brings tears to those who engage in the LifePlanning process. At the point of Life Gates they frequently come to see, "This was a sovereign act of God in my life."

Specific Lessons and Conclusions

God's guiding hand is often manifested in such a way through this construct that you come to these three great realizations about God and your relationship with Him:

1. God is always in relationship with me. The pattern of your life is not a series of isolated events in which God has acted as a manipulator or puppeteer. God moves in a flowing relationship with you, always wooing you closer to Him, never abandoning you, never completely letting go of you. You may struggle in the grasp of God, but God never lets go of you.

2. God is in command. Although you may think at times that you are doing your own thing or acting on your own, you never really are. You are part of a master plan in the mind and heart of God. He has you "on the line," and you are not capable of disengaging or hanging up on God.

3. God does not demand. You come to God of your own volition. He does not force you to communicate with Him, to praise Him, or to receive from Him.

A person once said to me, "I'm free, but I'm still in God's backyard." That's precisely the situation in which you find yourself. You cannot escape God's persistent call to pursue the life He has designed for you to live. You can rebel against it, and God will allow you to rebel even as He continues to call insistently with greater and greater urgency and volume.

Insights Are Both Immediate and Delayed

The insights that come during a turning points exercise can be profound. Some insights tend to come quickly. In many cases, I have seen people cry spontaneously as they see with a surge of insight how God has been at work in their lives. Philosophers refer to "the great aha" experience when someone has an insight into his own personality. This "aha" experience also happens when someone has insights into her creation and her uniqueness. The "aha" is not about self alone, however; it is about the nature of our awesome, omnipresent, all-loving, gracious God at work in a single human life.

Other insights come over time. Very often, a person will have new insights long after our sessions together. You may very well find that some insights come to you weeks, even months, after you have read this book.

I always give the time lines, charts, and matrices that are made during the LifePlanning process to the person who has come for a LifePlan consultation. One man told me that he reviews them periodically, hanging them on his home office walls for review just as we had hung them on the walls in my home office. The full picture of a time line that stretches over two or three walls has an almost confrontational impact. It's as if a mirror of his entire life to date has been held up before him.

GOD REVEALS HIMSELF THROUGH HIS AGENTS

Saint Thomas Aquinas wrote of "divine concurrence." His philosophy is a reality to me every time I facilitate a LifePlan. God intervenes in human life, most often by using other people as His agents.

As I facilitate a LifePlan for a person, I look for the presence of one or more of God's agents in his life. Very often this agent is someone who has been praying for him for years, even decades.

Several people have told me that a mother or an aunt or a grandmother never gave up praying for them in spite of their overt rebellion or their denunciation of faith. I have a growing respect for those who pray with diligence and endurance.

Saint Augustine was once a lecher and womanizer. Even his mother gave up in her desire to pray for her son, but God spoke to her heart, *Monica, continue to pray for him.* She obeyed, and she lived to see her son's character completely transformed.

You may find benefit in adding the names of various persons to turning point experiences in your life. In so doing, you will gain a greater appreciation for the role these people have played in your life and also a new appreciation for how God involves people in His plans.

In some cases, the person who has been used by God may initially appear to be the least likely person God *could* use—in your life or that of anybody else.

One of the most amazing stories I have ever heard while doing a LifePlan was told by a man who is very successful today. Earlier in his career, however, he had faced bankruptcy in his small town. He had been beside himself with fear and frustration at his financial demise.

One day the town drunk walked into his place of business, held out a book to him, and said, "You need to read this book."

The businessman said, "You can't even read. How do you know I need to read this book?"

The drunk replied, "I may not be able to read, but you need to read this book."

The businessman asked, "Where did you get that book?"

The drunk replied, "I got it at the drugstore."

"But you have no money. You stole it, didn't you?"

"Yes. You need to read this book."

"You stole this book, you can't read, you don't know what it says, and yet you tell me I need to read this book?"

"That's right."

"Okay, I'll read the book, and I'll pay the druggist for it."

The businessman began to read the book. After reading only the first chapter, he found himself out in Main Street confessing his love for the Lord. He was instantly converted. The book was *The Power of Positive Thinking* by Norman Vincent Peale. His life was changed dramatically, and as his life changed, so did his business.

The town drunk had been one of God's agents in the businessman's life.

There's no predicting how God will work in a life to bring a person to conversion or to surrender. He works through grandmothers who read the Bible to their young grandsons, through Sunday school teachers who are faithful in pursuing their students even when they fail to come to Sunday school, through intercessors who pray daily for the children in their neighborhood, and on at least one occasion, even through a town drunk.

Sometimes God's Interventions Are Dramatic

A woman told me how she had been used by God to be an agent to a woman in her community with a real gift for arranging flowers. Although it was far from her nature or habit to do so, she went over to the woman's house one afternoon and said, "I hope I'm not intruding by coming to your home, but my husband and I have seen some of your floral arrangements and we very much admire the work you do. Would you make arrangements for us on a regular basis? We'll pay you, of course, for whatever you bring us."

The woman answered, "I'd love to do that." She began to arrange flowers for the couple and to deliver fresh bouquets regularly. Two months went by, however, and the woman who had requested the floral arrangements realized that she hadn't received a bill.

She went to the home-based florist and said, "We couldn't be happier with the arrangements you are doing for us, but we haven't received a bill from you. We want to pay you."

The woman said, "You don't understand. You are my angel. I can't charge you."

The woman protested, "Oh, no, I'm not an angel. And I certainly want you to charge us!"

The florist said, "To me, you are an angel. The afternoon you came to my home and asked me to arrange flowers for you, I was suicidal. My husband had died. I was very depressed, and I had made all the arrangements to take my life that very night."

The woman who told me the story, usually a very private person, had never gone to another person's home to request anything, much less regular floral deliveries. But she followed God's prompting and a life was spared. She became God's agent.

Sensitive to the Working of God

God calls us to be aware that He is working through others on our behalf and also that He is working through us on the behalf of others. That is one of His most frequently employed methods—working through people to reach people.

I recently attended the annual conference of a major denomination in a city halfway across the country. Every night, we had a prayer service at the close of the business meeting. One night I sat next to a couple I didn't know. As the prayer service began, the wife said to me, "We don't know you, but I believe that God wants you to pray for us."

I said, "Terrific!"

We joined hands to pray. She said before I began, "My husband, who is a pastor, is without a church right now. We don't know where God is going to lead us. We're in transition."

I replied, "My son was a pastor. I know how tough it can be." I prayed that God's next assignment for them would become clear and that God's will would be manifested in and through their lives. We visited after the prayer, and I discovered that they lived just a few miles away from me. I was able to send them a book and write them a letter of encouragement when I returned home.

Later as I reflected on the experience, I realized it had not been a coincidence that I sat next to that couple on that particular night. It was no coincidence that we were almost neighbors, that I knew exactly what it meant to be "between churches" since my son had found himself in that position on more than one occasion, or that I understood about life's transition times and what it meant to trust God for His will to unfold. Our prayer time was a divine concurrence—a God-arranged encounter.

I have had many such encounters, on both the giving and the receiving sides. One of them came very early in my spiritual walk. When Debbie was ill, I answered a knock at the door one evening. The woman on our doorstep said, "Hello. My name is Kathryn Kuhlman. I don't know why I'm here. I don't make house calls."

I invited her in and led her into Debbie's room. I said, "This is why you are here." She was God's agent to us that night in her ministry to our entire family. God had brought one of the nation's most well-known ministers of healing to our door. She came in unquestioned obedience.

GOD DESIRES CHANGE AND GROWTH IN YOU

Certainly one valuable lesson that comes from spiritual discernment of your turning points and Life Gates is this: God desires change and growth in you.

Many people come away from this construct with a greater appreciation for what God desires to "put to death" in their lives. I believe that Paul was able to say that he was crucified with Christ because he had a very keen awareness and understanding that God had "put to death"—nailed to the cross—certain aspects of his former life. Certain sins, certain patterns of behavior, certain associations and affiliations, certain ways of thinking and feeling, and certain attitudes were to be no more. They were to be counted as dead and buried (2 Cor. 5:17).

> *Each one's work will become clear; for the Day will declare it, because it will be revealed by fire; and the fire will test each one's work, of what sort it is. If anyone's work which he has built on it endures, he will receive a reward. If anyone's work is burned, he will suffer loss; but he himself will be saved, yet so as through fire.* (1 Cor. 3:13–15)

You may gain a new understanding of what God does *not* want you to do, become involved with, pursue, or hold as an attitude. A turning points and Life Gates analysis can bring sharp conviction when you see your life differing from what you know to be God's commandments.

A number of people who have come to me for LifePlans have been caught in the clutches of what I call *a spirit of poverty.* They may have investment portfolios worth millions of dollars and high six-figure salaries; nevertheless, they have a strong fear of loss or of financial failure. They cling very tightly to what they have and to what they have achieved. Although they have a great deal, they are in the clutches of a spirit that tells them they are poor or on the brink of being so.

Jesus asked His disciples, who apparently were concerned about God's provision in their lives,

> **Consider the lilies, how they grow: they neither toil nor spin; and yet I say to you, even Solomon in all his glory was not arrayed like one of these. If then God so clothes the grass, which today is in the field and tomorrow is thrown into the oven, how much more will He clothe you, O you of little faith?** (Luke 12:27–28)

People who have a spirit of poverty do not possess money and material goods; money and material goods possess them. They are very afraid of opening their hands in generosity to give or part with what they have accumulated. Furthermore, people with this spirit never have enough. They tend to count every penny and are always on the lookout for those that they feel are cheating them or are dealing unfairly with them.

Many times in the course of facilitating a LifePlan I discern that a spirit of poverty has a hold on the person. Typically the person is unaware of this. God's spirit is one of abundance. A spirit of poverty is a spirit of infirmity. God runs a physical fitness center; Satan runs an infirmary.

The pastor who married Ginny and me said to me during our marriage counseling, "Should you want $16 million or sixteen wives?"

I responded, "Oh, I'd take $16 million."

He said, "Wrong answer, Tom."

"Why?" I said, dumbfounded that he would think sixteen wives preferable to $16 million.

He said, "Because if you had sixteen wives, you'd know you had enough!"

His point was well taken. People with a spirit of poverty are invariably greedy—their fear of poverty drives them to pursue *abundant* wealth, far more than what is needed. Having $16 million is never enough. At that point they want $30 million, and once they have amassed $30 million, they want $100 million. Greed is never satiated. It is a spiritual hunger driven by an unhealthy spiritual fear.

The pursuit of money over the pursuit of family, spiritual well-being, or community is very evident if people have this spirit and are honest in appraising their Turning Points Matrix.

Countless other such insights are the by-product of a turning points and Life Gates analysis. Ask the Holy Spirit to reveal to you *all* of the lessons He desires for you to learn.

GOD WASTES NO EXPERIENCE

God uses every experience of your life to bring you to a deeper understanding of Himself and yourself. No experience is a waste. Every experience has been allowed, if not directly authorized, by God.

Arthur Cushman McGiffert wrote this about the apostle Paul: "Paul's pre-Christian experience had been just such as to prepare him for that complete renunciation of personal merit and personal pride."[2] What may have seemed to Paul to be wasted years of rebellion and sinfulness against God's greater purposes for humankind were vital to his formation for the work God designed for him to do.

Could God have prepared Paul for his eventual ministry by any other means? Could Paul have come to a relationship with Christ *without* the stoning of Stephen or Paul's early years of very arduous theological training? Certainly—God is capable of working out His purposes in us quite apart from circumstances. What Paul experienced didn't bring him to the point of salvation. God's love and mercy and grace brought Paul to that point.

Even so, God uses every experience that we have for the working out of His plan. As someone said, "Nothing is ever wasted in God's economy." How amazing it is that God can weave anything and everything into the fabric of a plan that has goodness and blessing as its outcome. He alone is God!

Don't be dismayed as you reflect on the turning points of your life. God has been at work all along. He will use every experience of your past to position you for the fulfillment of your purpose in the future.

AN ABIDING MESSAGE OF HOPE!

Our God is a God of hope. What a believer gains from constructing a Turning Points Profile is nearly always a surge of hope that just as God has been at work in the past and present, God will continue to be at work in the future.

> ***We know that all things work together for good to those who love God, to those who are the called according to His purpose.*** **(Rom. 8:28)**

I have heard only once what I concluded to be the spirit of Satan speaking to my heart. His message was one of doom. His voice was ice cold and sterile in its monotone. Nothing in what he said or the way he spoke held any indication of life and, therefore, nothing of future—which is a key ingredient in hope. Satan's purpose is always to instill fear and to cause a paralysis of faith.

A Turning Points Profile helps you see that even in times of failure or error, God has provided a means for you to continue to live and to grow. This nearly always creates a strong awareness that God's plan is unfolding and that it is not yet complete in your life—in other words, God's plan is going to continue to unfold, life is going to move forward, growth is going to occur, and God's purposes are going to be revealed and fulfilled. In that there is hope!

IDENTIFYING THE PATTERNS, TRENDS, AND THEMES OF YOUR LIFE

As you look back over your turning points and Life Gates, identify patterns, trends, and themes.

Focus on meaning. Ask yourself,

- What did this mean to me?
- Why does this period or event have value to me?
- What were the critical consequences related to this event?

Patterns

Patterns are combinations of acts, qualities, and tendencies that form a consistent or characteristic arrangement.

A minister once came to me for a LifePlan, and his Turning Points Profile showed a pattern of consistently being put into positions of leadership but an equally consistent pattern on his part of refusing to accept the mantle of leadership. I invited him to see that his gifts were a sacred trust and that leadership was not a choice for him. He was called and installed to leadership by God. In the course of our time together, he accepted the mantle of leadership that God had placed on his life.

During the three years that followed his decision, his church experienced a tenfold increase in attendance. In accepting his role of leadership, he allowed a power to be released into his life. The Holy Spirit had been inhibited from working fully in him and through him because he had denied or thwarted the role of leadership God had planned for him. Once he allowed the Holy Spirit to work in him and through him as a leader who was embracing the leadership role, the move of God was powerful.

A pattern might be likened to a model. "Leadership offered, leadership rejected" was the model in that man's life that emerged from a set of actions, traits, and propensities.

Trends

Trends are the general direction, the prevailing tendency, the drift. The key words here are *general direction.* Look for the overall movement and the path being indicated across all turning points, and especially as the trend relates to the present moment.

A senior pastor who came to me for a LifePlan discovered during our time together that he was on a path toward burnout. He was a dynamic leader with the heart of an evangelist, and he never felt that a day was long enough or that enough had been accomplished. He worked around the clock, every day of the year. We both realized fairly quickly that he was heading at a breakneck speed toward a giant "end of the road" sign. Through the Holy Spirit's help, he felt he had permission from God to draw a line limiting the number of commitments he made and the activities in which he participated. He began to delegate authority to his staff members. His large church continued to grow, but he personally no longer felt chopped into fine pieces.

Themes

These are the dominant, recurring messages of life.

A number of businesspeople and ministers have come to me with life themes of finder, entrepreneur, leader, and builder. When they operate with their themes as central, they experience both inner emotional fulfillment and external vocational fulfillment.

These people often say to me, however, "I *can* be a second man." Sometimes they have slipped into that role, working as an assistant pastor, for example. They may be able to rationalize this role, but even so, the secondary role does not bring them complete fulfillment or deep-seated joy. The fact is, they are not in concert with the dominant theme of their lives.

One young executive and I determined in surveying her Turning Points Profile that she was gifted as a writer and concept developer. She was working as an administrator; in fact, she was the president of a small, thriving company. But her true life theme was as a creator, an originator, a thoughtsmith, and a wordsmith. The administrative work was a sidetrack for her and not central to the theme of her life. She immediately saw that she needed to relegate that part of her life to others in her company. Once she was free to engage fully in the creative process, she found more joy than she had ever experienced in her work and, ultimately, in all areas of her life.

Recognize the dominant theme in your life. Appreciate the importance of honoring its Source, God. Be true to the gifting. Dominant themes are always closely related to the gifts of God in your life.

THE PATTERNS, TRENDS, AND THEMES OF YOUR LIFE

Reflect about the patterns, trends, and themes you see in your Turning Points Profile. Consider the control path. Consider the Life Gates. Force yourself to engage in higher-level breakthrough thinking. Ask the Holy Spirit to give you spiritual discernment. Take time to ponder your life history.

Then draw some conclusions about what you see in your life story. Be gentle, forward thinking, and constructive in the conclusions you draw. Choose to embrace fully what God has done and is doing in your life!

Turning Points Profile
Meaning Summation

PATTERNS IN MY LIFE:

TRENDS IN MY LIFE:

THEMES IN MY LIFE:

As you prepare to leave this construct, recognize that one benefit of understanding turning points is the ability to recognize them *as they are happening*. All of us have twenty-twenty vision in retrospect. We can look back at periods of our lives and say, "If only . . . ," or "I wish I had . . ." The greater benefit comes when we can recognize a turning point in the present tense of our lives and say, "I now choose . . . ," or "I now act . . ." in a positive, self-edifying way.

Are you in a turning point right now? Are you perhaps experiencing a Life Gate?

8

MODULE #4: THE TALENT SEARCH

Our gifts are a manifestation of God in us. They are His gifts. They are the parts of His infinite and glorious self that He has chosen to implant into us for His purposes.

Many people today don't know who they are. They haven't found themselves. The key to realization about who you are is to discover your gifts. You then know the areas in which you need to grow.

In developing your gifts and acquiring mastery in them, you discover how best to apply your gifts. In all cases, gifts can be applied to serving others. The full application of your gifts through service to others gives satisfaction and fulfillment in life—it is the essence of feeling that you have had a meaningful life.

Show me a person who doesn't know his gifts or hasn't developed them for service to others, and I will show you a person who has little sense of purpose, meaning, motivation, and value.

In sharp contrast, the person who knows her gifts, has developed or is developing her gifts, is using her gifts to the best of her ability to serve others, as opposed to using them solely for selfish ends, and is using her gifts to offer the love of Christ to others *always* has a high degree of purpose, meaning, motivation, and value for her life.

How do you discern your talents? Your LifePlan will rarely present itself in large type. The clues are much more subtle. They are to be found in what you enjoy doing, in areas where you have known satisfaction, in achievements of which you are proud, and in your secret yearnings, drives, and affinities.

WHAT DO YOU *LIKE* TO DO?

A talent search begins in discovery of what you like to do and, beyond like, *love* to do with a passion.

I always encourage choirmasters to choose people for their choirs who are gifted in music. They will not burn out. Show me a person who has been musically gifted by God and I'll show you a person who will enjoying singing at any time of the day or night, until he no longer can utter a sound with his vocal cords. A person who loves music cannot get enough of music.

To a gifted musician, artist, writer, dancer, scientist, nurse, teacher, engineer—whatever the area of the gift—there is no sense of living fully unless the person is *doing* her gift. A person gifted to teach will find someone to teach, even if it's only a collection of stuffed animals lined up against the headboard of a bed. An engineer can't help making little drawings and scribbles that connect him to the world at large. A nurse will find someone to whom care can be rendered; a scientist will engage in some kind of testing of the world; a dancer will dance; an artist will paint or sculpt; a writer will write.

The problem many people face is that they have lost sight of what they enjoy doing. They have become so wrapped up in the expectations of others and the "necessities" that life has imposed upon them that they have lost sight of what they like to do.

WHAT ARE YOU *GOOD* AT DOING?

A second important key to talents and gifts is to discover what you are good at doing. The potential for mastery lies solely within your God-given giftedness. To discover your giftedness, ask, Where does my past success lie?

In building upon our example of a gifted musician, if a person's bent is music, he is capable of becoming a good musician. If a person's bent is *not* music, she may be capable of becoming an adequate musician, but never a truly good one. Becoming even adequate will require a great deal of practice, but no amount of practice will be able to overcome the lack of a bent in that direction.

Some people like a particular field but have no innate ability to succeed in it. Simply liking something, such as music, does not mean that a person has been gifted in music. A person who likes music may very well become a patron of musicians or may contribute behind the scenes to the furtherance of composition, performance, and musical technology, but he is wasting a certain degree of his God-given talent in the pursuit of a career that is *not* a gift from God.

I heard about a man who has an excellent ear for music, although he is not gifted as a singer and has never learned to play a musical instrument. Still, his ear for what is on pitch and performed well has given him a career in music—that of a sound engineer for a major recording studio. Is this man gifted in music? No. He is gifted with a very finely tuned ability to hear and to perceive differences in sound quality and pitch. He has turned that gift toward something he enjoys, music.

In sum, the gifted will always enjoy the performance of their gift. Liking an activity, however, does not always mean they are gifted to perform or work in that area.

The Key to Credibility

If people attempt to speak to others about practical matters that lie outside their giftedness, their words will sound hollow and may even become evil because they lead others astray. A gifted musician has credibility when he speaks about the practical aspects of music.

A gifted writer has credibility when she speaks about practical matters related to writing.

Those who are apart from Christ have no practical ability to speak about how to live a moral life. They may be capable of giving theories, but they should never be taken seriously on practical issues of ethics and morality. We have seen this happen time and again in modern history when individuals have spoken out about how to live a good or ideal life apart from Christ. In many cases, they have led others to an isolated life and eventually death. The life they have espoused has been anything but *practically* good.

We cannot deny that Hitler was a leader and a theorist. But in practice and in the application of his theories, he was a tyrant and an evil monster—a man far away from Christ, yet purporting to espouse the ideal society. He had no inner basis on which to tell others how to live. His thoughts, words, and dictates produced incalculable material destruction and human devastation.

Advice always must be related to what you are *in truth*. You are to live out who you truly are. You are to speak out of the reservoir of what you live. In that lies credibility.

YOUR GIFTEDNESS CANNOT BE CLONED

We are all aware of physical DNA and the way in which a particular set of genes is responsible for eye color, body type, and other highly specific physical traits, including, it appears, the predisposition of the body to certain diseases as well as the way the brain is organized to receive certain stimuli from the natural world. Physical DNA results in every set of fingerprints, footprints, palm prints, and voiceprints being different.

Genes are of a limited number in type, but the way they are combined and the sequence in which they are arranged give you your uniqueness.

In very similar fashion, your spiritual DNA is a precise combination, arrangement, and proportion of gifts from God. The result is that nobody

- will think the thoughts you think.
- will feel the precise feelings you feel at any given moment in time, in relationship to the given circumstances of a moment.
- will create what you create.
- will express himself or herself as you do through your non-verbal expressions and movements.
- will make the exact choices you make.
- will follow the precise sequence of experiences that you will follow in the course of your spiritual development and your growing relationship with God through Christ Jesus.

Everything about you spiritually (internally) is just as unique as everything about you physically (externally). Not only that, but God has placed you in a very specific family, given you a specific environment in which to live, and placed you in a very specific time frame in human history.

Given the infinite number of variables at work, it is really no surprise that you and your contributions to this world *cannot* be replicated.

Physical DNA may be copied or engineered to a certain extent, but spiritual DNA can never be copied or engineered. And spiritual DNA is the far more important feature of our individuality. It is the part of us that is eternal. It is the very essence of who we are for eternity. It is the basis for our contribution to the kingdom of God. Along with our historical, environmental, and relational uniqueness, our spiritual DNA cannot be cloned.

CONDUCTING A TALENT SEARCH

The Talent Search Construct is aimed at helping you discover your unique giftedness. The construct is presented here in chart form. Following it, we will define the terms of the construct.

THE TALENT SEARCH CONSTRUCT

TALENTS:

-
-
-

ELEMENTS	**EVIDENCE**	**LIFE DOMAIN MESSAGES**
CLUES:		
PASSIONS		FAMILY
NEEDS		
DRIVES		PERSONAL
OBSESSIONS		
CHARACTERISTICS		CHURCH/
QUALITIES		FAITH
LONGINGS		KINGDOM
HOPES		
ACHIEVEMENTS		VOCATION
		COMMUNITY
HEART:		
What do I care about?		
What do I dream about?		
My *opus gloria:*		
What will be my contribution?		

Clues

In the "Clues" section of the Talent Search Construct, you are to identify the traits that make you uniquely you. Start with any one factor, and write down a specific fact, trait, or quality. Identify at least one specific for each factor. Use as few words as possible to convey to you the specifics related to each factor.

For example, you might note these specifics:

Quality	Truthfulness
Drive	To Get Results
Achievement	Eagle Scout

Give yourself enough time for this process. Reflect seriously on what you really are and really want, need, or desire.

After you have identified at least one specific in each of the factor categories, go back through the list until you have two or three specifics for each factor.

> ***John answered and said, "A man can receive nothing unless it has been given to him from heaven."*** (John 3:27)

Don't force this process. And above all, don't write down what you think might be the right answer or the response that you'd like for another person to see. This is your opportunity to look into the mirror of your soul and personality. Be honest with yourself. Think about who you are.

I've provided explanations and questions to trigger in you a response for each factor.

Passions. Passions are what you cannot get enough of, what you want to do forever. Passions make work play.

Passion as used here refers to a depth and intensity of feeling toward a task, not a person. What do you most enjoy doing? In what do you most enjoy participating? In a television interview shortly before his death, the talented composer Aaron Copland said, "When you find what you are passionate about, you want to do it forever." I heartily agree!

I have found a number of things about which I am very passionate. I am passionate about strategic planning—I have an innate love of variables, the more the better. Over the years, I have become very adept at accommodating a great many variables. I love to synthesize them and develop a vision or comprehensive way of looking at them.

Some examples of passions are designing, creating, composing, healing people, preaching.

Ask yourself,

- What do I love to do?
- What can I *not* imagine living without?
- What makes a day or an experience more complete to me?

Needs. All of us have the same basic needs for food, water, air, shelter, security. We have a need for meaning and purpose in life. Beyond that, you have needs that are uniquely related to you. For example, you may have a need for space and orderliness. If things are too cluttered, you feel uneasy.

Examples of needs include music, affirmation, other people to work with, appreciation, encouragement, new challenges, sufficient personal space, being outdoors, and love.

Ask yourself,

- What do I need to have to feel as if I am able to function fully?
- What types of rewards do I need?
- What makes something worthwhile or valuable to me?

Be aware as you identify your needs that many people in our culture have been taught that they need far more things than they actually need. Our society says to us at every turn, "He who dies with the most toys wins." We are a society driven by the desire to acquire. Much of the violence in our society no doubt stems from this drive to have the possessions that we believe to be necessary for personal status, recognition, and approval.

Beyond the "toys" of material possessions, too many of us desire to acquire relationships in which we treat the other person as if he or she is a "toy." We play at being committed to other people in marriages, families, businesses, and churches.

A noted entertainer said a few years ago, "The heart wants what the heart wants." He was and is right. We emotionally crave what we personally desire. What we must recognize as being equally true is this: the heart has been taught from a very early age what it should want. Many people have had bad teachers. They have allowed billboards, media programs and commercials, advertisements, and unrighteous friends and family members to be the teachers from whom they have learned life's lessons.

It has been said, erroneously, that practice makes perfect. Bad practice only reinforces bad practice. Only perfect practice makes perfect. God's Word is very clear on what is right, what is good, and what constitutes perfect practice.

Drives. Drives are compulsions, not passions.

I am very opportunity sensitive or opportunity driven. If I see an opportunity, I move toward it immediately. I am always looking for new ways that a concept might be applied and be made useful.

My wife, Ginny, is problem sensitive or need driven. If she sees a need, she responds immediately. Given any set of facts, she immediately zeros in on what is missing or what might be a problem. She is a nurse by training, a career path that is very appropriate for a problem-sensitive person. In fact, you *want* a need-sensitive nurse, able to discern immediately any problem that may be in formation, including those that have not yet reached a dangerous, painful, or life-threatening level.

In communicating with Ginny, I couch my statements in positive terms. For example, I recently said to her, "We are going to Australia. You are going to love it. It's a beautiful country. You'll see koala bears and one of the most beautiful harbors in the world, and you'll meet some of the nicest people you will ever know." Her response was, "Thank you, Tom."

Had I said, "What do you think about our going to Australia?" Ginny likely would have responded with several reasons why we shouldn't go to Australia or why we should postpone our trip. They may have been valid reasons, but the net result probably would have been our staying at home. As it is, we went to Australia, and we have some wonderful memories of the experience. The mistake I made was that it was winter down under, and the cold and the rain made the trip far less wonderful than it could have been!

Opportunity decisions should not be submitted to a problem-focused person. Ginny appreciates my making these for her. In doing so, I am respecting and honoring who she is. I find this to be a void in marriages and relationships in general.

Some examples of drives are being results oriented, getting things in better order than you found them, making more money, and performing well.

Ask yourself,

- What motivates me to do my best?
- What causes me to choose right over wrong?
- What gets the gears going for me?

Obsessions. An obsession is something a person feels compelled to do or have. Without the desired object or relationship or accomplishment, life has little meaning and little quality for the person.

Examples of obsessions include fame, power/control, wealth, meaning, usefulness, and contributions.

Ask yourself,

- What do I seek to possess, do, or give at all costs (may be material, spiritual, intellectual, or emotional)?
- To what do my thoughts and desires inevitably seem to turn again and again?

Some obsessions are unhealthy. For example, a woman who has an obsession to be reunited with her former husband, even though he has remarried and so has she, is harboring an unhealthy obsession. In contrast, a woman who has an obsession to see her neighborhood rid of drug dealers may have a very healthy obsession, one that might compel her to a noble task.

The artist Monet became obsessed with water lilies. Patrons built him a retreat complete with a pond filled with water lilies and a home on the grounds. The world is richer for his magnificent obsession.

Characteristics. These are the traits that others see almost immediately in you. They are both inner (emotional, spiritual) and outer (physical, behavioral) qualities.

Some examples include being talkative, energetic, laid-back, quick-witted, slow talking, and self-righteous.

Ask yourself,

- What about me do strangers or acquaintances seem to notice first? What are their initial conclusions about me?
- If a person has had only a few hours of contact with me, how is he likely to describe me to others?

Qualities. These might also be called character traits. These qualities are innate to you; they are the product of what you have become or are becoming. Qualities cannot be put on and off like a suit of clothes. They do not change according to circumstance, presence of others, or situation. They are at your inner core. A Life Gate is a supra–turning point: a quality is a supra-characteristic.

Examples of qualities include giving 100 percent, being a family man, exhibiting integrity, and being trustworthy, outgoing, and a team player.

Ask yourself,

- If one of my close friends were asked to describe my character in one word, what is the word my friend would choose?
- What trait do I look for above all others in a friend or associate?

- How would I answer a person who might ask me, "What can I count on getting when I enter a relationship with you?"
- Which adjective describes me best?

Longings. These are yearnings, often unexpressed deep desires, or whispers of secret prayer. You might never have expressed your longings verbally, even to yourself. True longings are very likely to be yearnings that you have felt for many years or for as long as you can recall. They can lie very deep in the spirit.

Yearnings and longings are even deeper and often more vague than what we call dreams or goals. Many people I know have a goal of retiring with sufficient income to travel. They dream of seeing the world and living in a warm climate. The yearning that underlies these dreams and goals, however, is very likely a yearning to do something other than what they have been doing as a career. They have a longing for change that actually is a symptom of a deep inner dissatisfaction of some type.

People who are operating within their God-given purpose, doing what they know they were created to do, seldom think about retirement. Farmers who love to farm never think about a day when they won't farm. Painters who are passionate about their work can hardly imagine a day when they won't want to get out their paints and brushes and blank canvas. The same goes for sculptors, musicians, writers, teachers, and scientists, among others. I read about a physician who is still working well into her nineties. She sees a steady stream of patients on a daily basis; she is passionate about her work and has no yearning or longing to do anything else with her life. I also heard about a postal worker who is delivering mail in a rural area even though he is in his eighties. He works on a voluntary basis because he can't imagine anything more pleasurable to do with his days.

The person who has a strong dream of retiring and escaping to a different life has a yearning or longing for a change, for something other than what he has been doing. He should explore that yearning now, not so that he can retire but so that he can start working at something he truly loves to do!

The yearning for retirement may also be a yearning for more rest or play, or for more time spent with family members. The longing may be for more laughter, more times spent in intimate conversation with loved ones, closer associations with friends. That longing should be explored now, so these areas of life can be developed sooner rather than later. A new balance in life, a new emphasis on relationships, or a new prioritizing of schedules might be warranted.

Many times the gentle probing I have done to surface a yearning has resulted in my "giving permission" to people to incarnate their yearnings into words. In reality, it is the Holy Spirit's doing, for God is the sole Source of all good. Many lives have been greatly enriched in this way.

Examples of yearnings are to be free, to be self-determined, to complete a college degree, to feel accepted, to be respected, and to be part of a specific group.

Ask yourself,

- What do I most wish I had in my life that I do not presently have?
- If I could add just one accomplishment to my life, what would it be?
- What would I most like to do, change, or try?

Hopes. These might also be called expectations.

Expectations are what you expect the future to hold for you. They are where you hope to end up.

Examples of hopes or expectations include prospects for getting ahead, having a job, saving, being able to retire gracefully, finding growth and opportunity in a company, and having the company invest in your development.

Ask yourself,

- What do I hope to do in my life?
- What do I hope to be?
- What do I foresee as areas of future growth and accomplishment?
- What do I expect of myself?

- What type of Christian, friend, spouse, member, or participant do I believe I *should* be?
- What shortcoming most makes me feel as if I am a failure?

Achievements. Both personal and vocational accomplishments of which you are proud are strong indicators of who you are and the gifts you have, because for the most part, achievements reflect what you are innately equipped to do. For example, a person with many swimming trophies has been gifted with the physical abilities of strength, endurance, and speed in the water. A person who wins the typing contest in the secretarial pool is gifted with excellent eye-hand coordination, small-muscle coordination, and muscular memory. Even awards or victories that you may consider to be minor in nature can be good indicators of gifts.

Examples of *personal* accomplishments include peer recognition (election to office), a successful marriage, achievement of a college education while also working, and a community-service award.

Vocational accomplishments include a successful start-up, chairmanship of a task force that fulfilled its mission, a progressive track record of growth, and Employee of the Year Award.

Ask yourself,

- What is my foremost accomplishment to date (in my opinion)?
- What have I done that I believe is worthy of distinction or honor?

Qualities Overlap

In doing the Talent Search, be aware that qualities overlap. Don't worry about whether something is a need or an expectation. Make your best call. Passions, yearnings, and accomplishments are especially important because they are very strong indicators of gifts. The clues *as a whole* point toward your unique giftedness.

Take time now to list your specific clues and evidence on the chart.

THE TALENT SEARCH CONSTRUCT

TALENTS:
-
-
-

ELEMENTS	EVIDENCE	LIFE DOMAIN MESSAGES
CLUES:		
PASSIONS		FAMILY
NEEDS		
DRIVES		PERSONAL
OBSESSIONS		
CHARACTERISTICS		CHURCH/
QUALITIES		FAITH
LONGINGS		KINGDOM
HOPES		
ACHIEVEMENTS		VOCATION
		COMMUNITY

HEART:

What do I care about?
What do I dream about?
My *opus gloria:*
What will be my contribution?

Identify Your Foremost Talents

After you have completed the "Clues" section, turn your attention to the top of the Talent Search. There you will find three bullets. Write in those spaces the three specifics that can be derived from your list of clues and evidence that you believe *best summarize* who you are.

One woman who came to me for a LifePlan had noted these traits on her "Clues" list:

Passions: To be available to wipe away tears.

Needs: The hugs of children.

Drives: To make a difference.

Obsessions: To see children rescued from pain.

Characteristics: Intense; huggable; good listener.

Qualities: Enduring friend.

Longings: To help.

Hopes: To be a good mother.

Achievements: Four foster children helped through college, brought to Christ.

When it was time for her to note the three foremost factors of her overall talent, it was fairly easy for us to note together these things:

- Enduring intensity
- Commitment to children
- Compassion for those in pain

Can you see how we derived this brief summation profile from the specifics she had listed in her Talent Search?

Look for evidence of gifting by examining all of the clues. Don't stretch or force your evidence. From among the more than thirty items of specific evidence you should have identified, look for about fifteen or more pieces of like evidence before you are willing to conclude, "Yes, this is indeed one of my gifts." Don't take a single piece of evidence related to one of the clues and call it a gift. Use inductive logic, reasoning from the specific to the general. The gift of leadership, for example, is not going to be discerned from a single specific example related to one clue. It will be inferred through several specifics covering several clues.

What are the foremost talents that you believe God has given you?

Limited set. Don't be dismayed at this focus on only a few gifts or talents. A person usually has three or four dominant God-given gifts. We are not equipped for all tasks. Rather, each of us is gift equipped for mastery over something. If we grow and develop our set of gifts and we craft them through our life experiences, we will fulfill our purpose on earth.

In addition, we will always be passionate about our gifts. If we have found them, we will do them. We will not have to be prodded to perform. We will delight in our growth and in the doing of what we are gifted to do. We will experience purpose-driven lives.

Some people have developed a larger number of skills—perhaps through necessity or the influence of others. Even so, the genuine, God-given gifts are a limited set; they are the areas in which you can enjoy maximum success and effectiveness. Your focus needs to be on the gifts that God has given to you, not on the skills that you have developed through hard work or diligent practice.

The three or four gifts are all you will need; they are complete in themselves. No *essential* gift is missing. Look at your gifts. Are they complete? Do they comprise a whole? Do they provide potential for mastery? If they do not, perhaps you need to do further work on them.

HEART

Heart is where you are centered, where you desire to serve, the altar upon which you wish to place your talents. Giftedness is *what* you are. Heart is *where* you will most likely apply what you are.

Heart refers to empathy, attraction, or "draw" toward a group of people, a field of expertise, or a particular type of service. Evaluating your heart helps you determine where you best might use gifts, where you wish to serve, and whom you wish to serve.

> *There are diversities of gifts, but the same Spirit. There are differences of ministries, but the same Lord. And there are diversities of activities, but it is the same God who works all in all.*
> (1 Cor. 12:4–6)

The three questions to ask yourself in evaluating your heart are these:

What do you care about? What matters to you about whether it gets done or not? What about the status quo do you believe *needs* to be changed, and the sooner the better?

What do you dream about? What are your last thoughts of the day, your first thoughts in the morning? Remember, these are not general thoughts, but thoughts linked to specific locations, people, or situations. To what do your thoughts turn during idle or quiet moments in your life?

What will be your opus gloria? What will be your foremost contribution to humanity? What will you leave behind as your legacy?

Using the example of the same woman from the previous section, you might very well have anticipated her heart statements:

Care about: Seeing that abused children get help.

Dream about: Providing a home for a group of children recently encountered in a nearby neighborhood.

Opus gloria: Helping children to become loving parents someday to their own children (thus breaking a generational pattern of abuse).

Another person said that she dreamed about helping young people. She also felt a call to ministry. It was easy to see that her most effective area of ministry was likely to be a position that involved sharing the gospel with children or teens.

Respond to Your Heart

Reflect for a few minutes on what you truly desire, dream about, and hope to contribute to humankind. Then answer the heart questions on the Talent Search Construct.

Check Your Talent Search Against Your Turning Points

Turn back to your Turning Points Profile in Chapter 4. Do you claim to love children with your heart and yet have nothing in your "Clues" list that points toward your having children, being with children who are not your own, or being trained to work with children? If so, your claim to love children is likely to ring hollow. If you have no experience with children, your love for them is theoretical only. It isn't rooted in reality or practice.

A number of people are drawn to heart issues that they think they *should* have. They are issues that seem noble or that may currently be popular in our culture. In reality, however, they are not genuinely concerned about these issues. Be honest with yourself. Face up to what you *truly* have a heart for doing. Who do you truly want to serve with your life?

Gifts and Heart Go Together

Gifts (talent factors) and heart are intended to work together in your life. Your gifts equip you innately for service. Heart directs you toward an avenue of service in these ways:

Heart will direct you to a focus of compassion. Consider, for example, a person who has a gift of compassion for those who are in need. How a person applies that gift comes as the result of an intuitive answering of the question, Toward whom do I feel the greatest compassion? It may be toward the poor and dying, at which point the person may feel called to do the type of work that Mother Teresa did for years in Calcutta. It may be toward the ignorant, the sick, the starving, the emotionally wounded, the confused.

Heart will direct you to an age-group. A person who is gifted in teaching may have a heart for teaching young children or for teaching adults.

Heart will direct you to a subject matter. The person who desires to teach might teach the Bible, algebra, history, gymnastics, or any number of other subjects.

Heart will direct you to a location and a means of serving there. A young woman once told me that she felt called by God to be a missionary. She had a deep desire to share the gospel with others, she loved to travel, and she enjoyed being with people of other cultures.

"What will you do as a missionary?" I asked.

She knew her giftedness. She responded quickly, "Oh, I'll teach."

"What will you teach?"

"I'll teach English as a second language, including reading and writing English."

"Who will you teach?"

"I'm going to teach high school students. I've been teaching for two years, and I love to teach teenagers."

She had a heart for teaching, and a heart for a particular age-group.

"And where will you go as a missionary?"

"To China," she responded quickly and enthusiastically. "I've wanted to go to China ever since I was a little girl."

She knew her giftedness, and she knew her heart. She was very unlike another young person who also told me that he thought he wanted to be a missionary.

"Why do you want to be a missionary?" I asked.

"I want my life to count."

"Is that the only means of service by which you think your life will count?"

"No. But it's the best means of service, I think."

"Who has told you that?"

"Well, I've been interested in missions work since I was a boy." As I talked with him further about this, he told me that his grandfather had a strong interest in missionaries and that his father had once felt called to be a missionary but had not gone to the mission field.

"What would you do on the mission field?" I asked.

He was a bit taken aback by that question and finally said, "Well, I'd share the gospel."

"But in what means of service? A doctor, a bush pilot, a teacher, an administrator?"

"My college major has been accounting. I could help other missionaries with their bookkeeping."

"Where do you want to go?" I asked.

"Wherever God leads," he said.

The young man did not know his heart, and I suspect that he did not truly know his giftedness either. He had been told from childhood that accounting was a good field to enter because there was always a need for accountants, and thus he would always be able to get a job to support himself. He also had been encouraged from childhood to be a missionary, in part to fulfill the personal desires of his grandfather and father—not because he had expressed as a child an interest in missions work.

Furthermore, the young man had done nothing in his life up to the age of twenty to prepare for missions work. He had not corresponded with missionaries, become acquainted with missionaries, gone on short-term missions trips at his college, read about missionaries, prayed regularly for missionaries, supported missionaries, or even traveled beyond a radius of two hundred miles from his home.

Know your gifts.

Then know your heart.

What do you *want* to do? What is your heart's desire? To whom do you feel drawn?

Two people of the same general giftedness may have very different hearts. One person may choose to apply a gift to a need that is very narrow in focus, close to home, and impacts few people. Another person may have a heart to apply a gift to a need that is broader, far from home, and impacts many people.

A truly miraculous thing occurs when you dedicate your gifts to God's service—He anoints you for your mission, *His* mission, which you will execute. The mind cannot conceive where this will lead. You would be overwhelmed if you could foresee His plan. Your service will be eternal, adding your bit to the kingdom of God on this earth.

APPLYING TALENTS TO LIFE DOMAINS

Peter Drucker once said to me, "Everybody is good, but good for what? That's the question." That's the key. Talents are God's gift to us. What we do with them, our service, is our gift to God.

The next step in the Talent Search is to apply your talents—especially the three that you have identified as your foremost traits, coupled with your heart statements—to the Life Domains.

> *We are His workmanship, created in Christ Jesus for good works, which God prepared beforehand that we should walk in them.* (Eph. 2:10)

So often we see most clearly how to apply our gifts to personal life and to vocational life. Each gift, however, has an appropriate and highly beneficial application to *each* of the five Life Domains.

For example, let's assume that a person identifies a gift of giving wise counsel. She then must ask herself,

- How might I apply this gift to my children and to my spouse? How does this gift operate within the context of family? The gift of wisdom can be exercised frequently, but probably requires that open lines of communication be established between parent and child so that when a need or problem arises, a child thinks first of asking for a parent's wise counsel. I personally cherish those times when my children ask me to help them think through a situation that they face.

- How might I apply this gift to my vocation? Certainly a knowledge of how to do one's job is important, but wisdom is beyond mere knowledge. A person with this gift may seek to offer win-win suggestions, may serve on a committee that fields employee complaints and innovative ideas, and may volunteer to be a mediator between management and labor.

• How might I apply this gift to my church or faith community? A person may determine that he is too busy to take a full part in the operations of a specific church committee, but a person with a gift of wisdom may be able to give key counsel at the outset of a project. I have used my gifts in strategic planning to help the pastoral staff of my church anticipate and plan for upcoming programs and campaigns.

• How might I apply this gift to my community? The gift of wisdom may be beneficial to a neighborhood or town, on an individual or collective level. I am not involved in the political structure of my community, but I volunteer my services to several community businessmen to help them develop strategies for their small businesses.

I am a better father and spouse, church member, and citizen when I apply my giftedness to help others in the domains of family, church/faith kingdom, and community.

For our previous example person—the woman with a concern for helping abused children—the application was very straightforward. I've included her completed Talent Search. Note the application statement that has been added.

SAMPLE COMPLETED
THE TALENT SEARCH CONSTRUCT

TALENTS:
- Enduring intensity
- Commitment to children
- Compassion for those in pain

ELEMENTS	EVIDENCE
CLUES:	
PASSIONS	To be available to wipe away tears.
NEEDS	The hugs of children.
OBSESSIONS	To see children rescued from pain.
CHARACTERISTICS	Intense; huggable; good listener.
QUALITIES	Enduring friend.
LONGINGS	To help.
HOPES	To be a good mother.
ACHIEVEMENTS	Four foster children helped through college, brought to Christ.
HEART: **What do I care about?**	Abused children getting help.
What do I dream about?	Four siblings in nearby neighborhood need home.
My *opus gloria:* What will be my contribution?	Helping children become loving parents to their own children (breaking pattern of generational abuse).

LIFE DOMAIN MESSAGES

PERSONAL
Always have children around.

FAMILY
Have large extended family (foster care).

CHURCH/ FAITH KINGDOM
Start group home in context of church or nonprofit group.

VOCATION
Work in agency that helps abused children or start group home.

COMMUNITY
Teach parenting classes, give "adopt a child" opportunities to volunteers at group home.

APPLICATION: begin research about how to establish successful group home for needy children, within the context of church; meanwhile, seek to be foster parent for specific children.

This final stage of application involves the interpretation of the gifts, heart, and supporting clues into practical areas of work or tasks. The key question to ask yourself is this: How can I best apply my giftedness to each of the five Life Domains?

One person who came for a LifePlan was gifted as a musician. Her passions, her drives, her obsessions—as well as her longings and her accomplishments—all related strongly to her ability to play the organ. The traits that she wrote at the top of her talent sheet were these: musician, drive for excellence, precision, love of God. Here is how she related each of these gifts to the five Life Domains:

- *Personal:* Become the best organist I can be.
- *Family:* Involve my children in music and especially in church music but do not force them to participate beyond their giftedness.
- *Church/faith kingdom:* Use organ playing as means of helping others to worship God.
- *Vocation:* Teach and play organ within the church. (Note: she was already employed as a church organist and had just started accepting private organ students.)
- *Community:* Work with church staff to create concert series for community; provide two or three lesson times a week for students from poor neighborhoods who cannot afford to pay for lessons.

At times the mix of specific clues and evidence may not be as clear as in these instances I've described.

One of our facilitators did a LifePlan for a man who had widely diverse interests and desires. He had a passion for the outdoors. He was an excellent hunter and fisherman. He worked, however, in the sale of pharmaceuticals. An avid reader, he made it a point daily to spend time in both the Scriptures and the *Wall Street Journal.* He had fully surrendered his life to Christ in his early forties and came to the LifePlanning process desiring to make greater sense of what seemed to him to be unrelated interests in his life.

As he looked at his Talent Search and the specifics related to it, he saw a new possibility for his life. He realized that he had a deep desire to lead men's retreats as a means of evangelistic outreach and spiritual growth for the clients he served in the medical world. What type of retreats? Fishing and hunting trips! He envisioned ways in which he might share Christ with his clients in a recreational format, and he also could see that this might eventually become his vocation, not simply his avocation. Fortunately his wife was also an avid lover of the outdoor life, a good fisherwoman in her own right, and later, they began to dream of owning and operating a wilderness lodge devoted to spiritual retreats.

> *Having then gifts differing according to the grace that is given to us, let us use them.*
> (Rom. 12:6)

As you evaluate your Talent Search specifics, ask the Holy Spirit to direct you to the traits that are truly your outstanding or foremost qualities, passions, and interests. Ask the Holy Spirit to reveal to you how you might apply them in practical ways to each Life Domain.

DEVELOPING BOTH GIFTS AND HEART

The final step in consideration of your giftedness is to use the information you have gleaned from the Talent Search Construct and to identify the next steps that you must take to turn Life Domain applications into a reality.

Focus on the Tasks

In applying talents to Life Domains, you inevitably are faced with work, or tasks. Tasks are very specific and require skills. You must be gifted to do certain tasks and have a heart for doing them, and you must be able to do them. Enablement involves both inner enablement (the power of the Holy Spirit equipping and giving courage) and outer enablement (the acquisition of skills, abilities, knowledge, relationships).

Consider, as an example, a person who feels that he has been gifted to listen to problems and synthesize a solution. Such a person may make a very good counselor.

Counseling, however, is not an intuitive activity. It takes information, skill, and experience to become a wise counselor. Merely applying gifts to the vocational domain by saying, "I will work as a counselor," is not sufficient. He must focus on what *type* of counselor he wants to be and then face the requirements for becoming that type of counselor. The choice is far beyond whether he wants to be a psychologist or a psychiatrist. Virtually every professional field has a degree of counseling associated with it.

Lawyers are legal counselors. Within the medical profession, genetics counselors offer services far different from those of fertility counselors, although both are frequently involved in counseling couples who desire to have children. Teachers are often called upon to be counselors, and certainly school counselors may specialize in counseling that is behavioral, academic, or career oriented. Financial counselors offer advice on estate planning and the building of investment portfolios. Pastors provide a variety of counseling—spiritual, premarital, relationship oriented.

In determining which type of counselor to become, the person gifted for counseling must turn again to the clues of his giftedness and to his heart factors. They will point toward a more specific direction. In the end, he must choose a specific path with tasks that he enjoys doing.

A woman who is a writer shared with me a conversation she had with her father years ago. She was weighing two employment opportunities offered to her when she graduated from journalism school—to work for a major newspaper or to work in the public relations office of a Christian college. Both jobs involved extensive writing, which she loved to do and was innately gifted to do. Both held out promise for advancement and opportunities for growth in her talents.

Her father asked her to describe each of the jobs to him. She replied, "What do you mean?"

"What would you actually be doing, hour by hour?" her father asked. "Making coffee? Typing? Placing phone calls? Sitting at a desk?"

She hadn't thought of her role in terms of such specific tasks. She began to isolate specific duties and responsibilities.

In the newspaper job she would be sitting at a desk, rewriting copy that came over the Teletype machine, and making phone calls to get the quotes necessary to provide a local angle to the stories. Deadlines would be insistent and daily.

In the college job, she would have the freedom to roam the campus, conducting interviews and working with a wide variety of people in creating brochures, ads, catalogs, and magazines for the university. Deadlines would be a factor, but they would not be daily.

As she weighed the difference in tasks, her decision was readily apparent to her. She admitted to her father that she didn't like the idea of being chained to a desk or having the pressure of daily deadlines. She didn't enjoy doing phone interviews all that much. In contrast, she loved the idea of meeting many types of people in a college setting and of having lots of different writing challenges.

In our example about a person gifted to be a counselor, a person who enters the world of *financial* counseling will have much different daily tasks from those of a person who enters the world of *fertility* counseling. The person must ask, "Which daily tasks are most appealing to me?"

In the end, we gravitate toward tasks we enjoy. A gifted writer must enjoy not only seeing his work in print, but also generating ideas, writing them down, editing them and crafting them, cutting and pasting them together, and so forth. A gifted counselor must enjoy not only helping people with wise counsel, but also conversing, listening closely to others, doing research to support wise counsel, and so forth.

Consider the tasks involved in the doing of the gifts-and-heart application you have identified for each Life Domain.

Required Training?

Once you have determined to whom and in what field you expect to apply your giftedness, you need to ask, What type of training do I need?

In virtually all cases, a person never stops growing in the ability to learn how better to apply gifts. It's a lifelong process.

In the counseling example we used, the question to ask would be, "What type of training do I need to be the type of counselor I want to be?" The training is likely to include training in both a subject area (such as medicine, education, psychology, law) and counseling (which may be called by another name, such as client consultation or patient relations).

The application of your gifts may require different levels of training at different times. One level may be necessary for basic application, and then as your giftedness blossoms and develops, another level of training may be required for the gift to be of greater benefit.

I worked for two years in the controller's office of a major firm *not* so that I might become a "financial man." Rather, I wanted to learn the financial considerations of the executives for whom I conducted strategic long-range planning. I took courses at a university to prepare myself and to learn more about human behavior. That was not *necessary* for strategic planning consultation, but it was of enormous benefit to that consulting work and especially my Life-Plan consultations.

THE PURSUIT OF MASTERY

We are challenged by God to hone our gifts to the sharpest edge possible. Our gifts are given to us. We can choose to accept them or reject them, however. And most important of all, we can choose to develop them.

We are challenged to develop mastery with our gifts. This is what I call crafting our gifts. The person who is a master at a task is completely unconscious of doing a skill. A master pianist, for example, doesn't have to think about what notes to hit in the playing of a composition he has learned. A master typist doesn't have to think about hitting the keys of a typewriter; what the master typist thinks appears on the page without an awareness of fingers striking a keyboard.

Mastery Is Not Predetermined

When our daughter, Debbie, died at twelve years of age, a number of people, no doubt in an attempt to be helpful to us, told us that her death was "God's will." I rejected that concept then, and I reject it now. Those who truly hold to this position are determinists, referencing everything to God's unalterable blueprint for life. I am not a determinist, and especially so when it comes to the development of gifts to the point of mastery.

What God gives to each of us in a LifePlan is not a predetermined, cast-in-bronze, blow-by-blow plan. It is a general direction, a compass, a topical map to follow. He gives us the foundation of giftedness and a heart for applying that giftedness. He puts us into the contexts of family, vocation, church, and community. What we do with our giftedness and heart is our responsibility.

Mastery Is Rooted in Practice

Mastery requires the exercise of your gift—the *doing* of the gift.

The acclaimed pianist Paderewski practiced playing musical scales for four hours a day, even after he was recognized as being one of the foremost musicians in the world. He said that if he failed to practice for two weeks, he could tell a difference in his playing. A few more weeks, he noted, and the critics would notice the difference. And a few more weeks of not practicing, he mused, and the world would know he had not practiced.

What was true for Paderewski is true for all of us. Mastery is not a matter of wishful thinking. Mastery is rooted in practice and more practice and still more practice.

Believe You Can Become a Master

To succeed in the application of your talents, you must first believe that success is possible. The ancient Chinese general Sun-tzu wrote more than 2,500 years ago: "No good general ever started a battle that he hadn't already won." That's good advice for each of us!

If you are to win in the employment of your gifts, you first must believe that you have gifts and that you are capable of developing them to a level of mastery. "Mr. Average" is not a winner; he is an also-ran. The person who knows that he has gifts and then develops them becomes a genuine winner.

FOUR STAGES OF MASTERY

There are four stages in the process that leads to mastery of talents. They are stages of learning that someone theorized years ago.

Stage One: Unconsciously Incompetent

All of us begin the learning process at this level of being unconsciously incompetent. A toddler doesn't know anything about calculus. In fact, she probably can't pronounce the word. She doesn't know that she doesn't know calculus. She is incompetent in calculus but doesn't realize she is incompetent. She is unconsciously incompetent.

Stage Two: Consciously Incompetent

This is the realization that hits the first day of calculus class when a student becomes aware of all that he doesn't know.

Stage Three: Consciously Competent

A person can usually become consciously competent in most every general area of life he attempts to conquer. Greater or lesser effort may be required in some areas; a few specialized areas may lie beyond the realm of competency. But for the most part, most individuals develop a fairly high degree of conscious competency in life's basic functions. In our calculus analogy, conscious competency comes when a student studies calculus and earns an A on the final exam of the course.

Stage Four: Unconsciously Competent

This is the most exciting stage of all because it is the embodiment of true mastery. At this level, a person might complete a sophisticated engineering project, employing numerous calculus principles, without ever giving a second thought to mathematics. The level of unconscious competency is a wonder to behold in others. It is an exhilarating thing to recognize in oneself.

A Life of Mastery in the Spiritual Realm

Every person goes through these four stages in a walk toward spiritual maturity. We all begin at the unconsciously incompetent level where we do not know that we aren't living a righteous life. As new believers, we generally awaken to God's goodness and to the fact that we are not like God and are not living in the likeness of Jesus Christ. As we begin to practice Christian values more naturally and to obey God's commandments more willingly, we become consciously competent. The crowning glory comes when we begin to move into the stage of unconscious competence. At that stage, we live our lives in righteousness without thinking about every decision or questioning every motive.

A Lifelong Process

Gaining mastery is a lifelong process. No one becomes completely unconsciously competent in life. At every major stage of life, we tend to find ourselves back at the unconsciously incompetent stage. We have to learn what it means to be out on our own after high school or college, what it means to be married, what it means to be retired. Every crisis gives us an opportunity to face our incompetence. Life has numerous moments in which we are struck anew with the fact that we are incompetent and that we hadn't known that we were!

At each major emotional crisis in our lives, we also come back to the level of being unconsciously incompetent in our spiritual formation, although to a lesser degree than when we were unbelievers. We must learn again, "God loves me." Then we must discern anew His will and His purpose in the crisis that has struck us. Very specifically we must discover His "next step" plan for our lives. And then we must move into that plan and choose to live for Him and live out His plan.

Evaluate Your Progress

Periodically stop and ask yourself, At what stage am I in the mastery of the gifts I am seeking to develop? The logical next question is this: How can I move to the next level? What must I do?

In some cases the answer is practice, in other cases the move requires additional training or skill development, and in still other cases the upward move requires an update of an information base.

Don't become discouraged if you find yourself at a level that is less than unconsciously competent. Simply choose to grow! If we don't grow, we plateau. God plans for us to grow throughout eternity. As the Nike slogan says, "There is no finish line."

YOUR RESPONSIBILITY TO YOUR TALENTS

You are responsible for doing four things in response to God's giftedness and as part of developing your talents:

1. You Are Responsible for Choosing and Living Out Your Values

In whatever ways you choose to apply your giftedness to the Life Domains, you are responsible before God for an honorable, just, pure, and righteous application. Your values must govern all applications of your gifts.

Values are the baseline from which you make all of your decisions. If your values are not transcendent and lasting, they are the wrong values to hold. The Ten Commandments have stood the test of time, and they work in every culture and for people of all ages, both sexes, and of all income, education, and social levels. Furthermore they are values that help you become the best you can be. Any other values that you hold should bear these same qualities.

2. You Are Responsible for Your Faith Decision About Jesus Christ

You are responsible for being a witness to the saving love of Jesus Christ in whatever ways you choose to apply your giftedness in each Life Domain.

As a Christian, you are to apply your giftedness in living out in a day-to-day, practical way the life of Christ. In doing that, you truly are living. Anything less is a self-focused and shortsighted application of giftedness.

3. You Are Responsible for Focusing Resources Made Available to You

Focus is the convergence of resources on a purpose. In the realm of LifePlanning, your purpose is to do what you perceive to be the purpose of God for you, in you, and through you. You must bring all aspects of your life to bear on that purpose—time, energy, material resources.

> *Let us lay aside every weight, and the sin which so easily ensnares us, and let us run with endurance the race that is set before us, looking unto Jesus, the author and finisher of our faith.* (Heb. 12:1–2)

As a young man in my early twenties, not long out of college, I decided to focus on business planning. It was my conscious choice to become a master in that field. I didn't realize at the time how much I was playing into the hand of God's gifts to me. I simply sensed that I had found my vocation. I loved the strategic—developing plans, processes, and methods to obtain large goals.

My first assignment at the McDonnell Douglas Company was to help plan the DC-8, a plane that truly introduced jet transportation. There were far more unknowns than knowns—it seemed there were a zillion variables. Abstract entities such as "flat plate drag area" needed to be related to such practical entities as "operational cost per mile." The task of working on these plans was play to me. I was in my element. I loved every day of the project. And forty years later, I am still working at the craft I love, strategic planning, and I am still loving it.

Focus on my vocation led me to see my world differently. I related nearly everything I did to my business goals. The books I read, the courses I studied, the professional associations I made, were all geared toward helping me become the best strategic planner I could become. I focused.

A focused person behaves far differently from a person without focus. Life has much more meaning, much more purpose, much more intensity.

If we focus deeply enough, we bring the subject of our focus to a point of centeredness. This principle can be seen clearly in the way a lens can be used to concentrate and intensify the rays of the sun.

As I previously mentioned, many people have a career of starts. They never take the second step in any one thing that piques their interest or to which they turn their energies.

A person who is focused is very conscious about removing anything that doesn't contribute to her purpose. Extraneous activities, influences, and time occupiers are seen as waste.

A master gardener was once asked how he came to have the most beautiful trees on the block. The person asking the question intuitively understood that the process must lie in the pruning of the trees. The gardener responded, "I find the bent and remove anything that interferes."

The person who is focused on the implementation of a LifePlan is going to remove anything that does not contribute to living out that plan in the personal, family, vocational, church/faith kingdom, and community life dimensions. All time, talents, and energy will be devoted to achieving God's higher goals and purposes and to employing one's giftedness with love for the maximum amount of good.

Find the bent and remove anything that interferes.

Through focus, you can learn how to do every aspect of your chosen work as well as it can be done, and then, and only then, learn how to do every step as fast as it can be done.

I once watched a master carpenter at work. He was a highly skilled man. In talking with him, I learned that as an apprentice carpenter, he had learned how to do each aspect of his work with precision. At first, he admitted, his work was painstakingly slow. He made errors and learned how to correct them. Over time, he made fewer and fewer errors until he reached the point where his work was nearly flawless. Then he found that the more he continued to work at his craft, he was producing flawless work at faster and faster rates of speed. Finally he reached the point where he did not even think about *how* to do something. He simply did it—quickly, efficiently, and flawlessly. He had become a master.

4. You Are Responsible for the Commitments You Make

If you are to achieve mastery, you must become committed to your excellence, to the maintenance of your values, and to your witness for Christ. Focus narrows the field of vision. It gives you a row to hoe instead of an entire field to try to encompass. Commitment is the staying power necessary to ensure that you stay in your row and continue to hoe it to the end. Only the committed truly become masters.

Every Christian is challenged to make a pledge to self and to God that all will be done to God's glory. No one can force you to make such a commitment or to live by it. You are responsible for your commitment, promises, pledges, and vows. Make your commitments wisely, and only after asking the Holy Spirit for direction and counsel.

STRIVE TO BE AND TO DO YOUR BEST

Your ultimate goal in the development of gifts is to both be and do your best. You are to seek to develop your life to the mastery level in all of the Life Domains.

Being and doing your best, however, are not perfectionism. Perfectionism is related to an external absolute—an ideal of what it means to be best. It is always a shifting goal. The person who is locked into perfectionism always moves the markers, seeking to live without error and, therefore, without taking risks. Such a person usually gets very little accomplished. The book always needs to be edited one more time. The house never is clean enough. The product is never released for manufacturing. The perfectionist tends to get so caught up in details that she loses sight of the big-picture goals. And the perfectionist, by definition, always fails herself. What a downer!

Can any person get it right 100 percent of the time in every domain of life? No, of course not. Even masters make errors. But we can become progressively "more right" in all we do. We can practice our gifts, practice giving our gifts with love, and practice living in righteousness until we become masters at the Christian life. That is our higher calling. All of us are called. To *what* is the question.

PAUSE FOR REFLECTION

Do you have a new understanding about the person God created you to be? Do you have a clearer understanding of how you desire to apply your gifts to the whole of your life? Do you feel a new responsibility to development of your gifts and to their use?

Identify some of the next steps that you believe are necessary for you to take, based upon what you have seen in your Talent Search.

TALENT SEARCH REFLECTION

The most important step I can take immediately to develop my giftedness:

The most important decision I can make right now related to the application of my giftedness:

The most beneficial thing I can do to focus the application of my gifts in each Life Domain:

PERSONAL

FAMILY

VOCATION

**CHURCH/
FAITH
KINGDOM**

COMMUNITY

9

MODULE #5: DRIVERS AND COMFORT ZONES

What drives you? With what are you most comfortable? The answers to these two questions reveal a great deal about the way the Creator has shaped you.

A small and simple construct that I have used with a number of my LifePlanning clients is aimed at answering the question, What is in your frontal lobe? In other words, What moves you? and What comforts you? I have labeled these two categories as *drivers* and *comfort zones.* Within each category are three focal points.

DRIVER AND COMFORT ZONE CONSTRUCT

DRIVER	COMFORT ZONE
Power	People
Image	Ideas
Contribution	Things

Every person has a focal point driver and a focal point comfort zone. Each is valuable for the work of Christ on the earth today. No one driver or one comfort zone is more valid or spiritual than another.

Like talents, these driver and comfort zone factors are randomly distributed. You may have a different driver from that of your children or your parents. The same goes for your comfort zone factors. Learning to appreciate your driver and comfort zone, as well as those of others, can be an important step forward in your understanding of who God made you to be and for what purposes.

Drivers refer to the things that motivate you, that trigger you to action. *Comfort zones* refer to the things with which you have the greatest affinity—the things around which you experience the greatest sense of ease and familiarity.

DRIVERS

Drivers compel and propel action. Ask yourself,

- What excites me?
- What do I seek?
- What do I feel is a necessity?
- What do I crave?

People tend to be driven by three things: power, image, and contribution.

1. Power

These people wear easily the mantle of leadership. They can be controlling and manipulative in their exercise of power, but they need not be. Those driven by power include those who seek to empower others. In some cases, they are the power behind the throne—people who do not seek the limelight or the title, but who do seek to influence the choice about what is done, when, how, and with whom.

In a positive light, people driven by power desire change and see themselves as change agents. They are not satisfied with the status quo in their lives; neither are they satisfied with the status quo around them. The degree to which they love influences heavily the use of power in their lives—they can be tyrants and dictators, or benevolent leaders who bring help and growth to others.

Examples of people who are driven by power are Sir Winston Churchill, John F. Kennedy, and a company president.

To determine if you have power as the foremost driver in your life, ask yourself these questions:

- Am I most comfortable if I am the one in charge or if I can see that things are being done my way?
- Do I desire to make things happen, create momentum, or see that changes I desire are effected?
- Do I readily accept leadership positions when asked to assume them? Do I seek out leadership roles (as evidenced perhaps by running for an office)?
- Am I concerned about how and when I might earn a promotion or rise in rank or status within groups to which I belong?
- Do I desire to have greater spiritual power over evil, sickness, or things that plague humankind?

"Yes" answers to these and similar questions put you into the power category.

It's okay to be driven by power. Those driven by power can exert much influence for good. They can be stabilizing forces as well as growth forces in any endeavor, including the church.

Conversely, avoid the tendency to think that those who are driven by power are more important than those who are driven by image or contribution. Many power-driven people have a tendency to put down those who are driven by image or to take for granted those who are driven by contribution.

2. Image

To some people, what counts the most is the *way* things are done, especially the appearance associated with the way things are done. People driven by image are good presenters of a message, although they may not have been the originators of the message. They enjoy packaging people, ideas, and things. They turn their creative abilities toward the visual and the readily apparent.

People driven by image are generally very conscious of protocol, manners, appearance, and social acceptability. They often want everybody to be happy or everybody to be positive about the things, people, or ideas they present. They desire to please.

Examples of people who are driven by image include a marketing specialist, an actor or entertainer, a creative arts person, a fashion designer, and a public relations person.

To determine if you have image as the foremost driver in your life, ask yourself these questions:

- Is it important to me that I make a good impression?
- Do I care how things are accomplished as much as whether they are accomplished?
- Am I concerned with my appearance, including the image of my company, my neighborhood, my church, or the organizations to which I belong?
- Do I see "making an acceptable impression" as an important aspect of evangelizing lost souls?
- Do I readily accept positions related to publicity, design, decorating, or protocol?

- Do I admire those who perform well and who stay within traditional cultural boundaries, displaying good manners and social graces?
- Do I place a high value on public recognition and rewards for those who do good work, seeing both as necessary for inspiring others and building a good reputation for Christ?
- Am I as concerned about how my work is presented and perceived as I am about getting the work done?

"Yes" answers to these and similar questions put you into the image category.

It's okay to have image as your driver. Those driven by image can be very important in setting a stage so the gospel might be heard. They can be highly effective in wooing others to Christ and in preserving the beauty and traditions that are significant factors to many people in their development of a deeper spiritual life.

Avoid the tendency to think ill of those who couldn't care less about image. Many people who are image driven do not understand how those in power can *be* in power when they care so little about appearance or protocol. They tend to regard them as crass brutes, which may not be the case. They also have a tendency to be condescending to those who are contribution driven, thinking that they could be more effective if they only cared a little more about procedures, manners, social amenities, and appearance.

3. Contribution

People driven by a desire to serve or to make a contribution do not want to be in charge. They may have very little concern about how something looks or is perceived by others. They are driven instead by a desire to see goals reached and people helped.

Those who are driven by a goal of making a contribution may have a rumpled appearance because their focus is not on themselves, but on others. They often deserve a hero's badge, but if given one, they would quickly pin it on someone else. Their heartfelt goal is to help others succeed.

Examples of this type of person include Mother Teresa, a social worker, and a missionary nurse.

To determine if you have contribution as the foremost driver in your life, ask yourself these questions:

- Do I shun the spotlight?
- Am I uncomfortable being singled out, recognized, or made a fuss over?
- Do I care most of all that something good is accomplished, regardless of who does it or how it is accomplished?
- Do I find myself moving almost automatically to help others who seem to be struggling or in need?
- Do I find myself annoyed with what I perceive to be the materialism or fashion-consciousness of others when more "important" things are to be done?
- Do I prefer to be in frontline active service rather than in a decision-making role?
- Do I care more about getting the job done than about whether an awards ceremony or recognition dinner is planned after the job is finished?

"Yes" answers to these and similar questions put you into the contribution category.

It's okay to have contribution as your driver. Those driven by contribution are often unheard and unseen, working behind the scenes to get the job done. They can make a valuable contribution to any church group, missionary endeavor, or community outreach.

Conversely, avoid the trap of pride in thinking that because you are driven by a desire to contribute, you have special access to the high moral road. Don't think ill of those who are in power, since they may very well be the ones who provide the venue for the contribution you desire to make. Also avoid the tendency to disregard those who are image driven, thinking that they could get more real work done if they cared less about appearance.

Overlap

Some people may say that they are driven by more than one thing, but that is rarely the case. Own up to your driving force. Choose *one*, not because you think it is noble or because you *desire* to have that driving force, but because it truly is the force that drives you. Your Turning Points Profile and your Talent Search will confirm your choice.

Pride

As noted in each category, pride is not the property of any one area. The person driven by a desire to contribute can be just as proud as the power-driven or image-driven person. Rather, recognize that you have the driving force within you that you have, and then make a decision to use this force for good, and not evil; for expansion of the kingdom of God; for the benefit of others; and with love as your overriding quality, motivation, and attitude.

ALL FOR CHRIST, IN ALL—LOVE

Each driver can motivate ministry. Because we are Christians, our goal must always be "all that I am" and "all of Christ in me." We are to exemplify Christ's love in all that we do, aiming our driving motivation toward His purposes.

The power-driven person who is loving in his execution of power and who uses power to bring about good on this earth is a wonderful person to know, to follow, and to seek out as an employer. This type of power-driven person displays to others the awesome authority and sovereignty of almighty God.

The image-driven person who is loving to others and who seeks to do all things in a way that is beautiful, pleasing, and positive is a person who makes life more lovely and enjoyable. The efforts of such a person point us toward the beauty and majesty of God.

The contribution-driven person who works in love and humility is a person who displays the servanthood of Christ Jesus in a way that is compelling and life-changing. This person is always in demand—as part of every committee, every organization, every company. The work of such a person points toward the love and generosity of God.

You must be aware that others may be driven by forces that do not drive you. Their driving force is valid and natural for them, and if used in a loving, helpful, and positive way, their driving force is just as effective as your driving force. Encourage others to recognize their driving force and to embrace it and use it positively. Ask that they recognize that your driving force is valid and is also one that you can and do choose to use for the furtherance of God's kingdom on this earth.

COMFORT ZONES

We all have met people who are more comfortable tinkering with things in the kitchen than in mingling socially with their guests in the living room. We all know people who can get very excited about ideas and books, but who seem to have few social skills and even fewer abilities to deal with tools and gadgets. Some people care very little about people or ideas but are most at home experimenting in their labs, sketching at a drawing table, or concocting new creations at the kitchen stove.

This affinity is called the comfort zone. The overriding question to ask is this: In what setting do I feel the greatest sense of pleasure, satisfaction, and ease?

The three comfort zones are people, ideas, and things.

1. People

The person who has a comfort zone with people feels that relationships are far more important than either things or ideas. Such individuals tend to have strong emotions that they are keen to express; they rarely allow logic to override their emotions. Bonding with others is vital to them.

The person with a heart for people loves to be with people and seemingly can't get enough of people. Such a person tends to be a very good conversationalist, although shy and retiring people-affinity persons are content to sit quietly as long as they are in a room filled with people.

Those who are most comfortable with people take time to listen, are genuinely concerned for the pains and hurts experienced by others, and have an ability to rejoice with the joyous. They enjoy parties and social gatherings and are quick to show hospitality.

Those with a heart for people crave association and are very uncomfortable being alone. They often are troubled by a lack of people skills in others and may be very critical of a spouse, child, associate, or peer who doesn't seem to communicate well with others or who doesn't seem to have the same intense desire to relate.

Individuals with this comfort zone make excellent managers, counselors, and pastors.

2. Ideas

Some people live in the world of ideas. They love strategy and enjoy making paradigms and sketches. They are often very creative, expressing their ideas in the formats of music, painting, drawing, sculpting, choreographing, or writing. They are the theorists of the world—especially drawn to formulas and patterns and the ideas that prompt scientific experimentation.

In a group setting, they often appear to be daydreaming, out of touch, or to have poor social and communication skills. The fact is, their minds really are elsewhere. They are content in their inner world of thought and imagination. They see a world that is possible but perhaps not presently in existence.

All of their ideas need not be original. Some people who are most comfortable in the world of ideas are those who are able to polish, edit, or build upon the ideas of others. They give form and substance to the ideas of the pure theorists through strategies, plans, sequences, or procedures.

Individuals with an affinity for ideas often are writers, artists, scholars, inventors, strategists, or those who are involved in corporate development.

3. Things

The person who has a comfort zone of things is likely to feel emotionally at home tinkering in the workshop, sitting at the sewing machine, or working on the family car. A person with an affinity for things is often restless and uncomfortable unless he is doing something, generally involving the sense of touch or the use of hands. Such a person loves the feel of metal, wood, fabric, soil, or objects. She finds satisfaction in seeing something take shape, produce a physical or material result, or be fixed and put into good working order.

Those with an affinity for things enjoy being with other people only if the group is actively engaged in a task that has a strong tangible component, such as building a house. Ideas are important to this type of person only if they are directly related to something that is practical or tangible.

"Things" includes animals; those with this affinity enjoy grooming, riding, working with, and handling animals. "Things" also includes working with plants.

Individuals with this comfort zone often work as product designers, craftsmen, construction workers, engineers, tailors, chefs, or model builders. They also make excellent landscape architects, farmers, naturalists, florists, and veterinarians.

Identifying Your Comfort Zone

Most people find it fairly easy to locate their comfort zone. If you are unsure, ask yourself, What would be an ideal Saturday afternoon?

If you desire to go on a picnic with family and friends, you are likely to be a people person. If you would rather sit at home and be alone reading a book, writing a poem, or listening to a symphony on the stereo, you are likely to be an idea person. If you'd choose to be working in your garden or your home shop, or out riding your horse, you are a person with an affinity for things.

As in the case of drivers, no one heart focus is right or more noble than the others. Each has a strong role in the functioning of the body of Christ.

Those with a people comfort zone always make others feel welcome in the group. They are the ideal ushers, hostesses, and social planners within the church. They make people feel as if they truly are a part of the family of God. They are the heart, voice, and emotions of Christ's body.

Those with an affinity for ideas have the breakthrough insights into the Scriptures, often write the cutting edge treatises for the church, and come up with the innovative plans for solving the needs within a church body. They are the mind of Christ's body, the church.

Those with a comfort zone involving things keep the working plant of any church in order—from arranging the flowers for the weddings to repairing the roof and remodeling the church kitchen. They are often the first volunteers for projects, from helping elderly persons in the congregation with yard work to building the sets for the Christmas pageant. They are the hands and feet of Christ's body.

COMBINING DRIVER AND COMFORT ZONE

A driving force and a comfort zone are linked within you. They do not exist independently but come together in unique and creative ways.

The nine basic combinations are these:

1. Power—People
2. Power—Ideas
3. Power—Things

4. Image—People
5. Image—Ideas
6. Image—Things

7. Contribution—People
8. Contribution—Ideas
9. Contribution—Things

You no doubt can already see how these combinations might function.

1. Power—people. The person driven by power but with a comfort zone of people is going to be very concerned about how to marshal the masses. Such a person may very well gravitate toward politics.

2. Power—ideas. The person driven by power but with an affinity for ideas is going to want to make sure that the ideas are widely circulated and that they have maximum impact on the culture or group. Such a person may find an outlet in publishing or the academic world.

3. Power—things. The person who is driven by power and has a heart for things is going to seek to use machinery in the exercise of power. Such a person may be drawn to the military, to the use of heavy machinery, or to the use of computers or broadcast technology to wield power.

4. Image—people. The image-driven person with a heart for people is going to be very gifted in organizing large events for maximum pomp and circumstance. A royal wedding or a state funeral or a state dinner will be a desired challenge.

5. Image—ideas. The image-driven person with an affinity for ideas may be a fashion designer or the innovator of new packaging for an established product.

6. Image—things. The image-driven person with a comfort zone of things is likely to be an excellent landscape architect or window dresser.

7. Contribution—people. The contribution-driven person with a heart for people is likely to be drawn to group activities and efforts, perhaps working on medical teams rather than in solo clinical settings, or perhaps teaching groups of children or organizing the masses into demonstrations and rallies.

8. Contribution—ideas. The contribution-driven person who has a comfort zone of ideas is going to write the editorials that incite the masses to take on an important social concern.

9. Contribution—things. The contribution-driven person with an affinity for things is going to man the soup kitchen or volunteer to build the Habitat for Humanity house. In the corporate world, that person is likely to be an administrative assistant; in the church world, that person is likely to be a trustee or the church secretary.

Random Distribution

These nine combinations are randomly distributed among family members and organizational members. Each can be a force for good. The specific tasks and activities available to each combination are virtually endless. For example, the power-driven person with a heart for things might exercise his talents within a corporate structure or a church structure, within a branch of government or a school setting. Or she might be a union leader, a Scout leader, or the superintendent of a school district.

> *Cause me to know the way in which I should walk,*
> *For I lift up my soul to You.* (Ps. 143:8)

IDENTIFY YOUR DRIVER AND COMFORT ZONE

Now identify yourself on this construct. Circle the base force that motivates you. Then circle the thing to which your heart is drawn and for which you have greatest affinity. Identify your driver and your comfort zone.

DRIVER AND COMFORT ZONE CONSTRUCT

DRIVER	COMFORT ZONE
Power	**People**
Image	**Ideas**
Contribution	**Things**

Draw a line to connect the two areas you have circled.

REFLECT ON YOUR DRIVER–COMFORT ZONE IDENTITY

Reflect on what you have identified in this construct. Invite the Holy Spirit to reveal to you anything He desires for you to know about yourself:

- In what ways are you likely to express yourself?
- In what fields are you going to be most comfortable?
- What settings are you likely to engineer for yourself (including how you arrange your home, your office)?
- How are you likely to interact with other people?
- For what are you most likely to spend money?
- In what roles within the church are you going to find the greatest fulfillment and satisfaction?

One person who completed this construct as part of a LifePlanning process noted that she finally understood why her husband could often be found reading a book in the library of the home to which they had been invited for a party. She had chided him for years about not being social enough with others in a party setting. She exclaimed, "He has a heart for ideas! I'm the one with an affinity for people." The good news is that she also perceived that they were a good balance for each other since he often helped her see the big picture and long-range ramifications of a situation, while she helped him to see the emotions and communication dynamics that might be involved in the same situation.

Another person said after completing this construct, "I'm no longer going to allow myself to be criticized for being an image-driven person who has an affinity for things. Some of my friends have ridiculed me for being too meticulous. The fact is, I like for things to look beautiful and to be arranged in a neat and orderly fashion. It's my nature to adjust stacks of magazines and arrange furniture. I think I might be a good interior designer. I'm also the ideal person to help on the remodeling committee for the church social hall." Probably so!

Yet another person asserted, "I have always wished I was a contribution-driven person, at least until I did this exercise. I wanted to see myself that way. The fact is that I'm a power-driven person. I have a strong comfort zone with ideas. I need to explore ways of using both in creative ways to further the kingdom of God. That's where my *opus gloria* should and will be!"

Go back and take a second look at your completed Talent Search Construct. Your combination of driver and comfort zone may very well indicate other ways to apply your talents to each of the five Life Domains. What you ultimately choose to do in applying your giftedness should be in line with both the force that drives you and the affinity that you have for people, ideas, or things.

Know what's in your frontal lobe. Know what drives you. Recognize the zone in which you are most at home. Make the connection. Ask the Holy Spirit to reveal to you how you can use your driver and your comfort zone for His purposes, and how your combination of driver and comfort zone can have practical and beneficial expression in sharing the love of Christ with others. There is much to be done in God's kingdom, and it will take people with all nine combinations of driver and comfort zone to accomplish all that God desires.

10

MODULE #6: THE THINKING WAVELENGTH

The result of trying to function in a role for which you aren't mentally wired is going to be distress. I like to spell the word dys-stress because that makes it so easy to link to the word dysfunctional, *which is the ultimate outcome.*

Each of us is born with a built-in thinking wavelength—a way of organizing the world, tolerating change, and juggling variables. No one way of thinking is right or better. Thinking wavelengths seem to be distributed at random throughout our world, although these thinking wavelengths do not necessarily exist in equal proportions.

We must recognize that we have a thinking wavelength that may or may not be the same as that of the person we married, the person who supervises us, or those we supervise or with whom we routinely engage in tasks, conversations, decision making, or problem solving. A parent and a child may operate on different thinking wavelengths; in fact, some children seem to operate on a thinking wavelength unlike that of either parent!

Thinking wavelength is directly related to the work that you are going to do successfully. It is related to the way you need to prepare for, seek, and perform your jobs—both those related to income and those for which you volunteer. It is also related to the basic communication skills you need to acquire for use in family, church, and community settings.

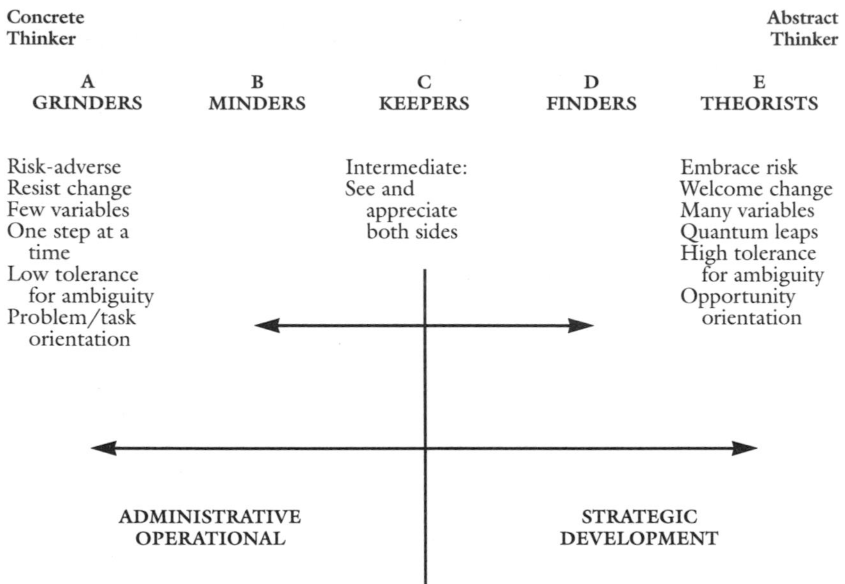

ORIGIN OF THE CONSTRUCT

Years ago, when I was much more active in corporate long-range planning, I had a client that was a world leader in the manufacturing of highly engineered products. The top-level administrators had difficulty controlling a salesman based in Europe, yet somehow he always seemed to be responsible for close to 50 percent of the total sales in whatever territory they assigned to him. He was considered one of their most valuable—albeit problematic—colleagues. The managers gave him progressively worse territories, and the result was always the same: a major turnaround.

Finally they assigned him to the Eastern bloc in Europe, the worst territory of all, and suddenly even that territory showed rapid improvement. The president was embarrassed because the Eastern bloc was then generating 50 percent of total European sales!

I asked *why,* and the company sent me to Europe to discover the salesman's secret. When I asked him how he accounted for his amazing success, he said to me in very simple and direct terms, "Tom, there are finders, grinders, minders, and keepers . . . and I'm a finder." I asked him to define the four classifications, and his definitions are the foundation for the definitions you'll find in this chapter.

He changed the way I thought about people. I later added "theorist" to the construct that man gave me and completed this construct as I am presenting it to you.

THE THINKING WAVELENGTH SPECTRUM

To help you find your thinking wavelength, here is more information related to each of the five categories. We'll move from left to right: grinders, minders, keepers, finders, and theorists. The flow is from concrete thinking to abstract thinking.

Grinders

Grinders get the work done. They are detail-minded doers. The world cannot operate without grinders. They provide the basic labor force for the entire world and all its operations. A company is likely to be successful only in direct proportion to the productivity, quality, efficiency, and morale of its grinders. They are the ultimate concrete thinkers.

Grinders have these tendencies:

- Document things
- Get the work done
- Are risk-adverse
- Like few variables

- Take things one step at a time
- Have a low tolerance for ambiguity
- Understand tasks and the need to solve problems
- Handle administrative details well
- Deliver working drawings

Positions usually best occupied by grinders include: corporate meeting planner, mechanic, administrative assistant, software programmer, bookkeeper, and line factory worker.

Within the church, grinders will build the sets for the church play, set up the fellowship hall for receptions and banquets, do the cooking, and stuff the envelopes.

Minders

Minders can manage a unit team, having both the people skills and the organizational abilities to do so. They can supervise the performance of work. They are basically concrete thinkers and are likely to function best in frontline supervision. They have an ability to conduct diagnoses and to problem solve. They will "mind the store" well, putting out brush fires upon their appearance.

Minders have these abilities:

- Can run a department
- Have diagnostic tendencies
- Are usually not innovative but perceive no reason to be
- Manage people in area of expertise

Positions often best occupied by minders are supervisor, teacher, chief engineer, section leader, and foreman.

Within the church structure, minders can be counted upon to keep the committees and programs of the church functioning. They will make sure the problems are solved and the details managed.

Keepers

Keepers are capable of managing the whole store. They possess an appreciation for the strategic and the administrative. They may have both concrete and abstract thinking skills, but will be biased to administrative/operational work. They make great mediators because they can relate to both ends of the thinking wavelength spectrum.

Keepers make good personnel managers, directors of departments, plant managers, and executive assistants.

Keepers have these tendencies and basic traits:

- Handle details and see the broader vision
- Handle variables well
- Are operationally biased, but have a sense of the strategic and appreciate the strategic side
- Are organized
- Are good with people

Sample positions that are good for keepers include department operations or division manager, chief operations officer, general manager, school principal, executive pastor, and academic dean.

Within the church, keepers are usually good staff associates, filling administrative duties related to the functioning of church programs. They are suited to be on the church board, lead home cell groups, or serve as committee chairpersons.

Finders

Finders open up new territory, close an important new account, reclaim a key lost account, or transfer new applications into a territory. They are entrepreneurs. Finders are abstract thinkers, so they often don't complete the paperwork that most concrete thinkers require. They can appear to be loose cannons within a group structure. They are innovators and creators. Follow-through is not their strength. They need grinders, minders, and keepers to follow in the wake of their creativity.

Finders can have these characteristics:

- Sense and seize opportunities
- Spot voids and fill them

- Are bored by a steady state
- Are good site locators
- Love a new challenge
- Must be thrown "raw meat" regularly

Sample positions often best occupied by finders include chief executive officer, chief visionary, product or market manager, joint venture leader, founding pastor, advanced development engineer, and entrepreneur.

Within the church, those who function in apostolic roles tend to be finders. They also are the ones most suited to be church planters and evangelists. They do well on the prospects calling committee and on the stewardship committee during funding campaigns.

Theorists

Theorists are bright, articulate, and persuasive, but in working with them, don't expect things to come to closure. Theorists can lead a company down a primrose path. They have a role best suited for universities, seminaries, and pure research laboratories. They don't belong in business. They cannot manage others well, and their ideas rarely become commercialized. Translation is not their thing. Theirs is a world in which the idea is the whole of it. In the proper environment, however, they can make highly significant contributions.

Theorists have these traits:

- Embrace risk
- Draw little sketches
- Can make quantum leaps
- Welcome change
- Are strategic
- Produce seminal concepts
- Enjoy many variables
- Are opportunity oriented
- Have a high tolerance for ambiguity
- Postulate the new, but don't execute
- Love the forty-thousand-foot macroview

Sample positions best occupied by theorists include scientist, researcher, and philosophy professor.

Within the church, theorists are the theologians.

Unfortunately they can also be cult leaders.

KEY CONCEPTS RELATED TO THINKING WAVELENGTH

Several key concepts are critical to understanding the thinking wavelength.

People cannot change their thinking wavelength, regardless of the amount or type of training received. There is very little potential for movement.

Don't burden others with decisions that are outside their thinking wavelength by more than one column. They will not be able to relate to your problem or to the solution you are proposing. I've seen this happen countless times. Grinders will say, "If I could just get to the top boss, he'd fix the problem." If the top boss is a finder, he won't know how to fix the problem, and he is likely to be reluctant even to admit that a problem exists!

In like manner, theorists have little capacity to understand why they must cut the budget of their pet research project.

Abstract thinkers may be able to do a concrete thinking job for a brief time, but they quickly will become bored with such a position and become very frustrated with the details.

Finders are quick to move from company to company, challenge to challenge. They often leave in their wake a pile of unfilled forms. Those who are their minders or keepers often feel as if they are going to go crazy in trying to tie down all the loose ends and keep their finders on track. Finders can't be nailed to schedules, protocol, or paperwork. Trying to do so is like trying to put mittens on an octopus.

A finder or a theorist will become more and more worn out and frustrated—with increasingly negative results—if he is required to do the administrative work of a keeper or minder. I have often seen serious illness as a result of such dys-stress.

The child who is an abstract thinker may be able to concentrate for a few minutes on picking up her room and doing mundane chores, but the chores probably need to be segmented into brief time periods.

Concrete thinkers are not able to engage in abstract thinking and will be overwhelmed if asked to do so.

Keepers often become frustrated when they ask grinders for suggestions about how to improve company functioning. The suggestions often seem to them to be petty and minute. Grinders, for their part, are only being true to the way they see things. They cannot think of corporate image, new protocols, or new ways of enhancing product appeal to customers. They will be expert at improving things in their own work or work units, however.

Children who are concrete thinkers need very specific instructions, generally given verbally. They need to be shown how to do tasks, as opposed to told how to do them.

People who are asked to perform a job outside their thinking wavelength will experience stress and internal discomfort.

Those who are operating to the right of their thinking wavelength are likely to feel what I term Stress A: frustration at *not being able* to do it. Those who are operating to the left of their thinking wavelength experience Stress B: frustration at *having* to do it. Both kinds of stress lead to eventual burnout.

> ***Gird up the loins of your mind, be sober, and rest your hope fully upon the grace that is to be brought to you at the revelation of Jesus Christ.*** (1 Peter 1:13)

BURNOUT PRODUCES AN IRREVERSIBLE CHANGE

What happens in burnout? Metamorphosis—a change in character, substance, and appearance.

People often come to me complaining of burnout. I point out to them that they may be approaching burnout, but they have not yet experienced it. The person who truly becomes burned out has undergone an irreversible change.

If a nurse burns out as a surgical nurse, she will never go into an operating room again. She will do pediatric intensive care, orthopedic, oncological, or some other form of nursing, but she will not go into an operating room. She will have changed to the point that surgeons, fellow nurses, and supervisors alike will recognize that she is no longer capable of being at peak performance in a surgical suite.

I have often counseled top executives about employees under their supervision, "You allowed this person to reach the point of burnout. You were insensitive to his needs and to where he was at in approaching burnout. Now is the time to deal sensitively with how you are going to reposition that person."

Executives frequently respond, "I'll give him time off—several months if need be. That should refresh him."

"No," I advise. "The person has burned out. That particular light cannot be lit again. He has no more value to you, or to himself, in that position or in that department. Find a new area for him. Find a replacement for his old position. The person's talents remain, but he has lost all motivation for doing his old job and he'll never be able to regain it. Burnout is an irreversible condition."

Some have tried very elaborate rehabilitation plans for burned-out managers and executives, but I have yet to see one of them work to the benefit of either the person or the corporation. Burnout is just what it says—the area has been leveled and is scorched. A new forest may grow—a new interest or challenge may be pursued after a period of rest—but the old forest is no more.

Horse or Burro?

Regardless of your thinking wavelength, you also have a propensity toward how much work you are likely to take on. The question I often ask in LifePlan consultations is this: "Are you a burro or a horse?"

We live in an area where burros run free. In my reflecting upon these burros one day, I realized that every client I have ever had in the corporate world had both horses and burros on staff. Do you know which you are?

A horse accepts every assignment, takes on all work, says no to nothing, and is very likely to burn out, become ill, or even lose his life in the process. A horse will die under the saddle or break his wind, which is the equivalent of burnout. Some CEOs who are not sensitive to this tendency have allowed some of their key people to assume more and more duties to the point of overload.

Burros are smarter than horses. They refuse to get into overload. Put too much on the back of a burro and it will sit down. It won't move! A burro knows when enough is enough.

Burros, of course, can be frustrating to CEOs. They say no to excessive overtime and extra responsibilities. In the end, however, they are the more stable faction of the workforce.

Horses tend to be the 5 percent of the workforce that creates 50 percent of the profits. In the end, however, they have much shorter life spans within a company. With their greater turnover as a group come greater training and personnel development costs, recruiting fees, and severance pay costs. If you are a CEO or the leader of a group, weigh the consequences. Don't let your horses take on too much. Keep your burros motivated to work at maximum level.

On the personal side, recognize which you are. If you are a horse, you will need to pace yourself and give yourself permission to say no to some projects, some promotions, and some commitments. If you are a burro, recognize that you are likely to need to prod yourself to test your limits and then to maintain a maximum workload without overload. Horses must learn to restrain themselves and take a vacation. Burros must learn to motivate themselves.

Give Yourself Permission to Say No

I remember a man who came to me for a LifePlan, and very quickly I realized he was absolutely exhausted—physically, emotionally, mentally, spiritually. He could not give himself permission to say no to the many responsibilities he had taken on in his life. The responsibilities were ones he thought he had to assume when, in fact, they were ones that others had manipulated him into carrying. The total of the responsibilities was too heavy for any one person to carry. To make matters worse, he was a perfectionist.

This man felt guilty for staggering under the heavy load on his shoulders, but even when he recognized that he had taken on too much—far more than was humanly acceptable and certainly far more than was required of him by God—he still was unable to let go. I finally said, "I give you permission to let go of these responsibilities."

I repeated this permission statement several times, and finally, with tears streaming silently from his eyes, he said, "Okay." He had to be given permission by another person. Fortunately he was able to receive that permission and later to act on it.

If you recognize that you have taken on too many responsibilities, too many obligations, too many burdens of others, and you find yourself unable to let go of any of them, I give you permission right now to do so! Tell yourself and anybody else, "Tom said I didn't have to do all this."

God never gives us responsibilities that will drain us of all energy or destroy a domain in our lives.

IDENTIFY YOUR THINKING WAVELENGTH

The Thinking Wavelength Construct is presented again here so that you may locate your thinking style on it.

THINKING WAVELENGTH CONSTRUCT

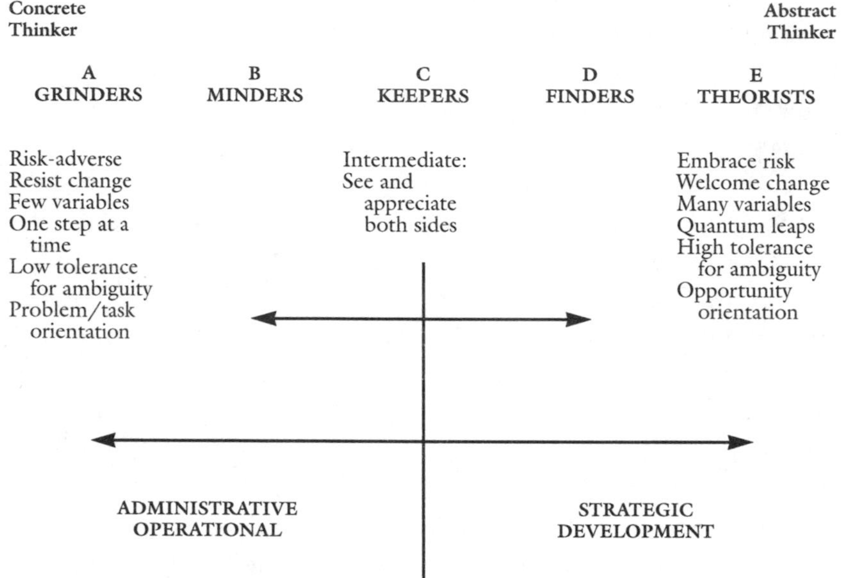

Now, ask yourself these questions:

- Where does my current job description fall on the thinking wavelength spectrum?
- Does my current job description match my thinking wavelength?

If your thinking wavelength and your current job description do not match up, start planning for a change in job. You can change your job. You can't change the way you think.

Your job may have a span—it may not be a single point. But unless the center of gravity of your work peaks at your thinking wavelength position, you will be in stress. A visionary trying to be a keeper will be a very unhappy camper. He will need a life balancer, an assistant to manage the details. This releases the visionary to be himself, to make his contribution in an optimum way. A job that is drifting out of his joy zone is a big warning signal.

Switching Is Better than Fighting

An old ad campaign had as its slogan, "I'd rather fight than switch." No! When it comes to thinking wavelength, you are better off switching than fighting.

Let me give you three examples of those who agree with me.

In the mid-1970s the chief executive officer of one of the largest and most widely known companies in the world assembled a task force to go throughout the nation to discover how entrepreneurs think and work. The company had lost its entrepreneurial edge. I gave this advice: select a sales branch and identify the finders within it. Put them into finders' work. The company selected a branch that had sixty people in sales. All were screened to identify the true finders, who were given frontline sales positions and worthy rewards for securing new accounts, reclaiming lost ones, and opening up new product territories. The results were so profound that the company conducted screening in every branch of the company. The positive outcome turned the company around.

A director of evangelism for a major church denomination came to me for a LifePlan. He told me that for every one hundred churches he had planted, less than seventy were still in operation five years after they had been planted. He was dumbfounded as to how to resolve the problem. I asked a few probing questions and then said, "You are putting keepers or minders into the work of finders. Keepers and minders are maintainers; they don't start up new enterprises. They can manage growth, but they are not true builders. Put finders into the churches you plant. They'll build up the churches. Put keepers and minders alongside them to do the administrative work. Don't expect one person to fulfill both roles." He did so, with a much higher rate of success.

Dave Bright, the former CEO of one of the largest training companies in the world, the National Education Corporation, and I had lunch three years ago shortly after he had retired from his position. He said to me, "The most helpful advice that you ever gave me was, 'Get the right person in the right job and the problems will melt away.' It took us five years, but we implemented this principle from my direct reports all the way down to first-tier supervisors." In nine years, the company's business went from $9 million in sales to $500 million.

It's Not Too Late

I once facilitated a LifePlan for a man who had been in the wrong job for twenty years of his thirty-year career. We had plotted each of his jobs over a wide range of posts on the Thinking Wavelength Construct. I said to him as we completed the exercise, "You can't change the way God made you to think. But you can change your job."

He voiced remorse that he had wasted so much of his life doing what he was not gifted to do—tears flowed for the wasted years. I said, "Don't look back. Look ahead. Change now and do what you *are* gifted to do." He took my advice, and within months, he had found a new position more suited to his thinking wavelength. He was making less money, but he was far happier and he noted, "I'm not earning as much, but I'm also not spending as much on medications, vacations, and various therapies that I thought were necessary to help me with stress. My quality of life has actually gone up."

His morale was also much higher. When he had been in a post ill-suited to him, he was highly criticized, and he accepted the criticism as his personal failure, although he didn't know why he had failed. In doing a job suited to his thinking wavelength, he was experiencing success, validation, and praise.

PAUSE FOR REFLECTION

Take a few minutes now to reflect on what you have learned about yourself in this module. Ask yourself,

- What action do I need to take regarding my thinking wavelength and the work that I do, the volunteer positions I fill, or the roles that I have taken on?
- In what ways may I need to adjust my expectations regarding others?
- In what ways do I need to adjust my communication with others?

- Do I have a tendency to take on too much work and put myself in overload? If so, what changes do I need to make?
- Do I have a tendency to say no when an opportunity seems overwhelming? If so, what do I need to do to make sure that I don't miss an opportunity for good that God has planned for me?

Remember that no one way of thinking is best, right, or desirable. Accept who you are and the way you think. Accept others for the thinking wavelength given to them by the Creator.

Remember, too, that God made both burros and horses. He has made you for a capacity to work. Find it, fill it, but don't exceed it.

Think about the majesty of God's plan to ensure that all work needed to get done does indeed get done. Not only does all work get done through the random distribution of giftedness, but it gets done when it needs to get done, during the day or at night. The Source of all is God.

11

MODULE #7: TRANSFORMATION THROUGH SURRENDER

We are not today what we were yesterday. We will not be tomorrow what we are today. We are in the process of being changed. This change for believers is not the change of mere difference, but a transformation. We are becoming like Christ.

I watched my little girl, Debbie, be transformed into a saint. When she was eleven years old, she was diagnosed with cancer of the spine. That was in the 1960s, long before the more effective treatments we have today. Debbie's health declined quickly and with a relentless increase in pain and suffering.

She spent the last few weeks of her life in a little hospital room that we created in our home. We had around-the-clock nurses at her side to care for her and to administer oxygen and pain medications. We did everything we could to fight back death and ease her agony.

During the final weeks of her life, Debbie made a concerted effort to apologize to people who came to her bedside for virtually anything that she thought she might have done to hurt them or disappoint them. She was not healed physically, but she nevertheless was made whole by the process of asking for and receiving forgiveness. Even though her physical health declined, God forged her spiritual well-being.

I do not believe for a second that God caused Debbie's disease or her death. I do believe that God can use any situation, even one as morbid and as terrible as Debbie's, for the furtherance of His plan. Out of Debbie's illness and death, her father was saved. In His great mercey, God went further. He gave me absolute proof that Debbie was now in radiant health and happy. I'll share more of this one day. The God of all comfort (2 Cor. 1:3) fortified my life when my heart was breaking. The life of our family was transformed over time into one that was truly reflective of God's generous love.

I came to a new understanding that God has a plan for each one of us and it is for our good—for our inner peace, for our total prosperity, for our spiritual transformation.

The Process of Transformation

The process of transformation is never complete in a lifetime. I believe it will continue into eternity. I find it very exciting to think that I can continue to grow in my faith and in my responses to life so that I am transformed by God more and more into the likeness of Jesus Christ. What a possibility! How wonderful it will be to one day be able to think and feel and respond just as Jesus Christ thinks, feels, and responds.

One of the best-known models related to human psychological and sociological growth is Abraham Maslow's hierarchy of human need.

MASLOW'S HIERARCHY OF HUMAN NEED

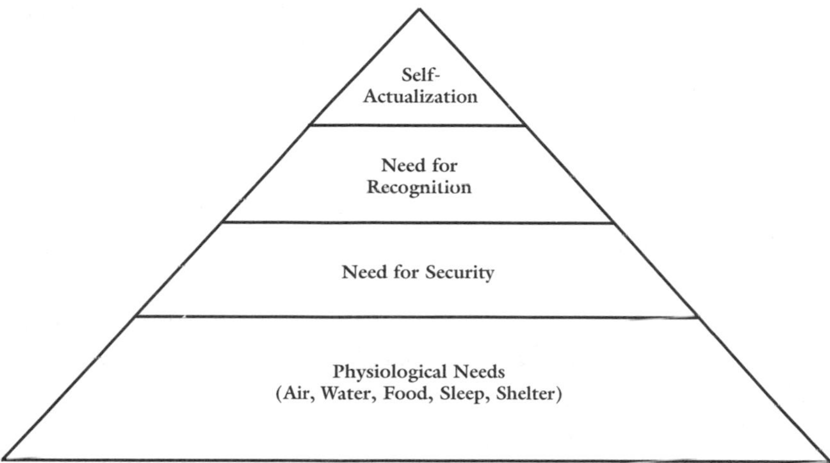

Maslow's basic premise was that we human beings cannot rise above the fulfillment of lower needs. For example, a person's primary needs are for sufficient air, water, food, sleep, and shelter. Deprivation in any one of these areas will become an all-consuming need in the person's life. Little else will matter.

Once the basic physiological needs are met, the next concern is for personal safety. The result tends to be the building of safety structures and the huddling together of people in order to enhance chances of security against the natural elements and war-seeking enemies.

Only after both physiological and safety needs are met can a person be concerned with receiving recognition for individual effort. The person who does receive such recognition then can move to the pinnacle of human need—the need to pursue one's potential and one's full reason for being. Self-actualization (or self-realization) is the full release of human potential.

The contention is made that if a major emergency arises—for example, a natural catastrophe threatening one's home, or a major illness threatening one's life—the person is reduced to that level of need meeting.

In our world today, with a massive number of white-collar executives still in the permanently temporarily unemployed category, a large segment of a very talented population that was once at the self-actualization point is suddenly reduced to the level of seeking security. People who remain behind in the downsized companies also tend to struggle at the recognition level, although they, too, know what it once was like to live in the self-actualization zone. The result of being pushed down to a previously met level of need can be frustration, panic, fear, and depression.

It is helpful to recognize where you might be on Maslow's hierarchy of human need, and even to recognize *why* you are there so that you might focus on what is truly important and not become frustrated with what once was. It is also important to recognize that the meeting of the need is what counts. A shift in job title, a relocation to a smaller house or town, a switch from white collar to blue collar, or the move from a corporate office to an entrepreneurial enterprise is not what truly matters. What matters internally is having your needs met: physiological, safety/security, and recognition.

Acknowledging the Spiritual

Abraham Maslow did not deal with spiritual transformation. His model is strictly a psychological-sociological one. As Christians, our concern must be for the whole, which includes the spirit. While it is helpful to know where we are in our psychological, emotional, and sociological growth, it is even more beneficial for us to have a model that deals with the spiritual process of growth, change, and transformation. In Romans 12:2, Paul wrote about transformation: "Do not be conformed to this world, but be transformed by the renewing of your mind, that you may prove what is that good and acceptable and perfect will of God."

Each of us is a spiritual, emotional, mental, and physical being. In our Western civilization, we tend to isolate those areas of our lives—labeling them spirit, emotions, mind, and body—and then to examine them as if these categories occur naturally and in reality. The greater fact, however, is that we cannot be divided in this way. You cannot tell me about your spiritual life without describing to me what you feel and think. You cannot tell me what you think without revealing to a certain degree how you feel. All of your expressed thoughts and feelings reveal something about your spiritual state. You are "one."

Part of becoming a whole person lies in recognizing that you have been created as a singular being, with each aspect of your creation related to all other aspects. It is as if you are a multifaceted cut diamond—each facet capturing and radiating a degree of light, but all facets part of the same stone.

The spirit is ultimately the integrating influence of all other facets of your life. It is the essence; it is the everlasting aspect of your being, the overriding ruler over every relationship you have.

When the spirit is tuned to self, and self-centeredness is pervasive, your thoughts and emotions cause you to relate to other people and to the physical and material world in self-absorbing ways.

When the spirit is tuned to God, and Christ-centeredness becomes pervasive, your thoughts are no less directed, your emotions no less ruled, your relationships no less impacted, and your relationship with the physical and material world no less important, but the influence of the spirit is 180 degrees opposite that of a self-centered spirit.

You are transformed *entirely* when your spiritual focus is transformed from self-centeredness to Christ-centeredness. You truly are a new creature, a new being. Your responses, desires, goals, thoughts, feelings, purchases, physical concerns—all undergo a radical transformation the longer you walk with Christ and the deeper your relationship grows with Him.

Spiritual Transformation

The spiritual transformation process is essentially one from being a sinner to being a spiritually mature Christian. It might be charted in a way similar to the model used by Maslow, except that I have inserted an important concept: surrender.

SPIRITUAL TRANSFORMATION MODEL

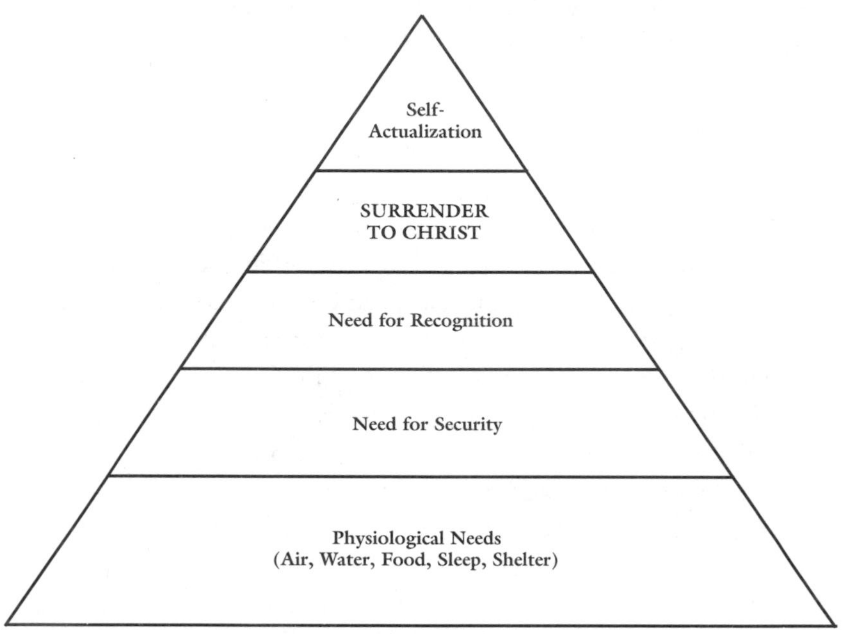

I do not believe it is possible for a person ever to fully actualize the self without a complete surrender to Christ Jesus.

As surrendered Christians, we are separated as vessels for God's exclusive purposes. We do not live unto ourselves. We are His. And His work is to transform us into the likeness of Jesus Christ. That transformation results in our being fully actualized as God's creations. It is in surrender to Christ that we truly find fulfillment and deep inner peace and contentment.

The fully actualized person according to Maslow is seeking to live up to his mental, emotional, and physical potential. The self-actualized Christian is seeking to grow in spiritual potential through a process of pouring out self more and more, and allowing more and more of self to become filled with Christ's presence.

CONVERSION IS RARELY FULL SURRENDER

The surrender process begins with conversion, but it does not end there.

Salvation (Conversion)

At the point of conversion a person comes into relationship with God through a belief in Jesus Christ as God's Son and an acceptance of Jesus as having made the one complete and definitive sacrifice for the forgiveness of sin. Jesus becomes the Savior of one's soul.

Conversion marks the beginning of the development of the spiritual being that has been latent to this point. There is a reception of the divine Spirit of God into one's life.

Conversion alone, however, is not surrender. Surrender means submitting all of oneself to Christ; nothing is withheld.

Surrender

At the point of surrender, a person makes a complete renunciation of confidence in self and claims a total reliance upon the presence and power of God. A practice of Christlike behavior, attitudes, and responses becomes paramount. The person has a passion to walk with Christ and to be completely Christ-centered. The person generally has a revelation of the greater mission that God has for her. The surrendered believer seeks to become fully engaged in God's purposes.

> ***Being confident of this very thing, that He who has begun a good work in you will complete it until the day of Jesus Christ.***
>
> (Phil. 1:6)

Up to this point, a person may have had a feeling of Christ living within on a sporadic or periodic basis, but the completely surrendered person lives in the revelation of "Christ in me." The converted person remains in something of a struggle between the carnal and spiritual person. The surrendered person has come to the point where this struggle ceases—the spiritual person has won out. Christ becomes the supreme role model. Love becomes the prevailing hallmark of the person's life. God speaks directly to the surrendered heart, building a personal and intimate relationship with the person—revealing His desires, His longings, His plans.

It is my contention that only the surrendered person is going to fully embrace God's plan and purpose, and is going to make a commitment to living out God's LifePlan. The converted person may gain perspective during the LifePlan process, but the converted person also is likely to perceive God's plan with the thought, *Let's see if this works to my benefit.*

The surrendered person, in comparison, will regard God's plan with the thought, *I know God's way will be for my highest good.*

You must recognize where you are in the process. If you haven't surrendered your life fully to Christ Jesus, you are going to find it very difficult to fully accept God's LifePlan for you, and you will find it equally difficult to maintain a commitment to the fulfillment of God's plan.

HAVE YOU FULLY SURRENDERED?

In my more than thirty years of doing LifePlans many people claimed to be fully surrendered to Christ, yet as I gently probed areas of their lives, they nearly always admitted withholding at least one area. In many cases, the unsurrendered area made them just as frustrated and discontented—lacking inner peace—as those who made no claim to have accepted Christ into their lives.

For some, a career or material life stood in the way of full surrender. For others, something from the past—a hurt or problem that they continued to hold on to and to cultivate—stalled full surrender.

One man told me very bluntly, "I'll fully surrender my life to God when I retire." He had a high income, and he wasn't prepared to abandon it. He believed that in surrendering his life fully to Christ, his income would drop and he would be in need—or perhaps better stated, want. He equated a full surrender of his life with a loss.

Take some time to reflect on your spiritual life. If you have not come to the point of full surrender, you may still have some recognition needs that you need to face. You may have some inner emotional work to do to prepare you for that step.

What I do know with certainty about surrender is that if people choose to make this step, the Holy Spirit is a ready ally. His comfort and presence are profound, and often are manifested in very dramatic ways to those who surrender fully to God.

THE CHOICE TO SURRENDER

An opening of self to spiritual self-actualization is a matter of choice, of becoming intentional about your life. God calls you to surrender, but He does not force you to surrender.

What Keeps Us from Surrender?

Certainly one major factor is fear. Many people don't believe God will take care of them if they surrender all of their will and their desires to Him. In truth, God gives us our breath, our heartbeat, and our life energy. We cannot be our own defense, provide for ourselves, or be our own safety. God alone is our refuge. Deuteronomy 33:27 solemnly states,

> **The eternal God is your refuge,**
> **And underneath are the everlasting arms;**
> **He will thrust out the enemy from before you,**
> **And will say, "Destroy!"**

Another enemy of surrender is our pride. Ultimately it is *the* enemy. Augustine confessed to this attitude: "I want to be good, but later, not now." We want to do what *we* want to do before we are willing to give ourselves to doing only what God wants us to do.

Always an Element of Struggle

It seems to me as I have read the history of the saints through the ages that all of them experienced a period of suffering. Through suffering, we realize we cannot, are not, and will not. We will fail despite our best efforts to succeed. We will fall short solely because we are finite creatures living in a fallen world.

Paul described the conflict and tension that we experience as part of our struggle against surrender to God: "I see another law in my members, warring against the law of my mind, and bringing me into captivity to the law of sin which is in my members. O wretched man that I am!" (Rom. 7:23–24).

Paul went on to ask the question we inevitably ask, "Who will deliver me from this body of death?" and then he answered that question from his position as a fully surrendered man: "I thank God—through Jesus Christ our Lord!" (Rom. 7:24–25).We cannot resolve our anxiety, deliver ourselves from our stress, or manufacture peace for our souls.

For each person, the details of surrender are different. I don't know what may have a hold on you or what you may be holding on to. I do know that when you make a full surrender, you will know it, and you will admit that you have not been fully surrendered in the past. Surrender requires spiritual *and* emotional readiness. I believe that, by and large, the church has missed this. The church needs to help people come to know God and help them know how to live: the spiritual *and* the practical living out of the Christ-centered life, as individuals, as families, as the brotherhood of men.

The Price of Surrender: Denial of Self

There is a price to be paid for becoming Christ-centered. The fully surrendered life requires the denial of self. This is a high price for us since, from birth, we are self-centered people.

One fact of life that we are wise to recognize is that virtually all of our problems are rooted in self-centeredness—problems in marriages, problems between parents and children, problems in industry, problems between employers and employees, problems between producers and consumers, problems in government, including problems between governments on the international stage.

Self-centered individuals produce self-centered families; they, in turn, produce self-centered communities; and they, in turn, produce self-centered nations. The ripple effect is automatic and irreversible.

Describe for me any problem on this earth—from a personal friendship to the highest level of international politics—and I will show you self-centeredness at work.

The good news that Christ holds out to us in surrender is that a positive pattern can be created. Christ-centered individuals produce Christ-centered families; in turn, those families produce Christ-centered communities; and those communities produce Christ-centered nations. The new normalcy to which God calls us in surrender is to yield to what God desires. In that we will experience forgiveness, reconciliation, restoration, wholeness, and a self-emptying in service to others. There is no problem on earth that can not be solved when that pattern is put into effect.

You must settle the matter for yourself and answer the questions, Do I stay in revolt? Do I continue to attempt to resolve all things by myself and live unto myself? Or, Do I submit my life to Christ and allow Him to indwell me with His presence and transform me into His eternal likeness?

Your surrender of your life to Christ is the greatest gift you can ever give to yourself or to God. Friendship is the gift of self to another. God desires a relationship with you, that of an intimate friend. You give yourself to Him, and He gives Himself to you. Christ says, "Give Me your heart; I'll come and live within you." And when that occurs, a relationship is forged that makes failure impossible for you. You have a relationship with the infinite, all-powerful, and all-knowing God, and He never fails. We are still little wires, but we are plugged into the Infinite Power Source.

The Freedom to Surrender

God created us in His image, not as automatons. He created us to be determiners, not to be determined. He created us to be programmers, not to be programmed. He created us to have dignity and the capacity to extend dignity and respect to others. We are not puppets. We are to be actively involved in God's ongoing creative process on the earth. Through Christ in us, we are cocreators.

Here are some of the precious freedoms that God offers to us through His grace as we *choose* His upward calling:

The freedom to accept His invitation to follow Christ or reject Christ. Jesus is the sole path of life among the many primrose paths that proclaim, "This way to the good life." Jesus said that He *is* the door. He is the way. He is the truth, and no one comes to the Father except by Him. We have the choice to take Jesus at His eternal word or to deny Him (John 14:6). He promises to show us the path of life.

The freedom to be free of guilt through accepting what Jesus did on our behalf in being crucified and resurrected. The Cross is our means of becoming free of guilt and the shame of our sin. It is our means of receiving the gift of the Holy Spirit. It is our means of being awarded the gift of eternal life and of experiencing an abundant life on this earth (Rom. 3:24–25).

We cannot possibly love ourselves as much as God loves us. God is not the author of condemnation. Jesus clearly said that He did not come to condemn the world, but that through Him the world might be saved. God offers us love, affirmation, and validation.

Until you accept that God loves you as much as He loves His only Son, Jesus, you cannot fully accept yourself. And until you accept yourself, you remain your own jailer. A tape will play continuously in your heart and soul, "Guilty as charged." You will continue to be a master of self-criticism, heaping condemnation upon yourself.

The freedom to live the abundant fullness of life or to live in true poverty of spirit. True poverty is never finding God and, therefore, never finding oneself. We gain true riches when we empty ourselves of self and open ourselves to receiving the fullness of all God offers to us.

We have been fed a lie by the world, which tells us that material wealth defines us. Such a philosophy is the epitome of the self-centered life. That philosophy creates a poverty of spirit that will result in our being sick with a moral disease that is at the heart of all human conflict. We become possessed by our possessions.

The mystery of our faith is that when we empty ourselves of our wants and replace them with what God wants, we enjoy an abundance of things that matter the most to us: love, fellowship with others, joy, peace, health, wholeness, and everything of lasting benefit. We are given a richness in the things that money cannot buy and that no one can achieve on personal merits.

Ask elderly or sick persons what they value most in their lives and they will probably tell you: my health, loving family members and friends, an inner peace, the ability to laugh, a feeling of purpose, meaningful work. These are things that cannot be purchased. They are gifts from God, the Source of all good, freely given in greatest abundance to Christ-centered people.

The freedom to learn, accept, and hide God's Word in our hearts or to ignore it. We cannot find God or come to know Him in the abstract or through the words of learned people. A relationship with God is built through personal involvement with God—reading His Word, talking and listening to God from the depths of the spirit, and seeking to follow God's commands and to rely upon His presence in every situation, every circumstance, every decision-making opportunity, every challenge. Genuine freedom comes when we partake of God's Word as the manna of life—relying on it as food for spiritual growth and development.

The freedom to develop a personal, intimate relationship with God or to attempt to go it alone through life. Being alone with God is never being truly alone. When we are alone with God, we enter into an intimate relationship with Him that is beyond description in words. We live in His presence, and by His Spirit, moment by moment. Life becomes whole and meaningful when we come to that level of relationship with God. Things hold no fascination for us, and we have no attachment to them. People are vastly important to us, but they do not dictate our actions, and they are incapable of manipulating us spiritually or destroying us emotionally. We do not cling to others out of a desperation to experience love, for we have the unending and unconditional love of our heavenly Father.

The freedom to become all that we can become, to rest continuously in the process of becoming throughout eternity, or to close down and refuse growth, development, and the very concept of potential. God desires to lead us into the fullness of the life He has willed for us, and to equip us to enjoy that life and be successful in it. The life that

He unfolds before us, however, is never ending. We will not fully arrive in the course of our years on this earth. We will remain "under construction" all of our days and throughout all of eternity.

The joyous mystery of this life in Christ is that the more we grow and develop in our giftedness, the greater the opportunities God gives us to use our giftedness, and thus the greater the challenge to continue to grow and develop. The Bible speaks of God's "enlarging our tents"—calling us always to enter into a greater and greater possession of our souls and to greater and greater applications of our ministries.

The freedom to accept the graces of God or to reject them one by one. When we become sensitive to the boundless ways in which God has cared for us and continues to care for us, we are humbled before His awesome love. We have the choice either to humbly accept God's freely bestowed gifts, knowing that these gifts are not awarded to us on our merits, or to reject His gifts because we have chosen to attempt to earn gifts of our choosing.

God's gifts to us are at His discretion. They are pure, eternal, and always for our highest good.

The freedom to spend eternity with God, walking in His paradise, or to choose a life apart from God, which is hell. Life or death? That was the choice that Moses placed before the people of Israel, even as he called to them, "Choose life!" A full life or a half life—an abundant life or a life of fragmentation—that is what Christ offers us. (See John 10:10.)

Each of us has the opportunity to choose freedom. As for me, I choose the way of the Lord: the path of freedom, the fullness of life made possible through His grace, the capability to soar in my spirit and, ultimately, to live the life I am meant to live.

PAUSE FOR REFLECTION

Ask the Holy Spirit to reveal to you what He desires for you to be. Ask Him to show you His path for becoming the person with whom our heavenly Father wants to spend all eternity. Ask Him to reveal to you what He desires to cleanse, purify, and transform within you. Then respond to His desires with thanksgiving and act upon them.

As you reflect on your life, ask yourself,

- Am I willing to yield all to Christ? To yield my will to His will?
- Am I willing to accept fully Christ-in-me?

Full surrender is yours for the asking and seeking.

12

MODULE #8: THE GIFT OF HELPFUL RELATIONSHIPS

God's gifts to us come in a variety of forms. Some of His greatest gifts to us are people. He allows for us to enter into and to develop certain relationships that are for our growth, development, and blessing.

I know that I could never have become what I have become in my life without the wife God gave to me. I met Ginny when I was fifteen. My father advised me to play the field. My response was, "I am going to marry Ginny." I never wavered from my position. I had fallen in love for life.

Most fifteen-year-olds may not know their divinely chosen mate. I knew mine. Ginny has been my most loyal cheerleader all of my life. Our love has grown to a depth and breadth neither of us could have imagined when we met at fifteen. All along the way, we have felt that God *intended* for us to be together. That doesn't mean that life has been easy at every turn. We have been through difficulties and tragedies in our family. Certain times in any marriage are more blissful than other times. Yet through it all, we have had a keen awareness that God brought us together and that we were a gift to each other.

I am keenly aware, and have always been aware, that God gifts us with relationships. He blesses us with and through people.

In many relationships, opposites attract. The reason, I believe, is that two people can come together to be a more perfect whole. Each fills in the missing pieces in the other person's personality. The extrovert draws out the introvert, and the introvert calms the extrovert. The generous free-spirited soul brings excitement to the more closed, pensive soul. In return, the closed, pensive person compels the generous free-spirited soul to take the important things in life more seriously.

When it comes to our giftedness, we are wise to seek out those who have complementary gifts—gifts that mesh with ours and fill in the gaps that we are missing. Such people can be tremendous assets to us, and vice versa.

COMPLEMENTARY GIFTS

I once consulted with the premier division of a software company, which was producing more than 50 percent of the company's total sales and profits. I led the division leadership through the strategic planning process, and at the conclusion of our time together, they had cheered their own plan. When the applause died down, the vice president of the division invited me to come to his office.

He said to his secretary as we entered his office, "I don't wish to be interrupted for the next half hour." He closed the door behind us.

We sat down, and he looked me in the eye and said, "We just finished a great plan for my division."

I said, "Yes. It is really a great plan. It's a good mosaic. It will go very well."

He said, "I appreciate that this is a great plan. I value strategic thinking. But I can't think strategically. I want to run this company someday. How am I going to do it? I can't think the way I need to be able to think."

I said, "You don't need to think strategically. But the company needs a great strategy, and therefore, it needs a good strategist."

"I know," he said.

"You don't need to change a thing about your role. You are a superb operational executive—in fact, one of the very best I know. You have been shaped just that way and to make just that contribution."

"How are we going to develop great strategies?" he asked.

I said, "We are going to put someone alongside you as a staff aide who is a great strategist and who can do what you cannot do. That's how we're going to do it, and that's how you are going to run this company someday."

> ***We, however, will not boast beyond measure, but within the limits of the sphere which God appointed us.*** **(2 Cor. 10:13)**

Fortunately for me, I was working with the company CEO on another project, and I had already identified just the strategic thinker that this executive needed to work alongside him. Some years later this man was promoted to CEO and he has been running the company successfully for several years. The company has grown to the point that it generates about $5 billion in sales each year, and this premier division some $4 billion of that.

This man is an acknowledged success—doing precisely what he was shaped to do. Part of his success lies in the fact that he didn't try to do what he was not created to do. He works well with his staff aide who provides the strategic thinking that *he* has been gifted to provide; the staff aide is not gifted to be an operational executive and has no desire to be one. Together, each man functioning within the parameters of his giftedness, they make a superb team. The strategist staff aide is a life balancer, releasing his boss to fully bring his giftedness to play and to maximize his contribution.

Partners in Giftedness

I have seen this model of pairing or partnering giftedness work time and time again.

Many people have sat with me in the LifePlanning process and have said to me in various ways, "What a relief!" There is a tremendous sense of release when a person recognizes that she does not *need* to be gifted in all ways that a certain job description may demand. Others can fill in the gaps and find fulfillment in their lives as part of the process. The overall direction is forward and upward. Usually the two people working together can generate far more than the two of them working alone.

The pastor of a very large church once said to me when he realized his giftedness, which included discernment of what he was *not* gifted to do, "I can't tell you how good this feels. It's as if a huge load has been lifted from my chest. I thought I had to be an administrator. I'm not gifted to be one. What I need is to find a good administrator—one who truly is gifted by God in administration—and work with that person."

People frequently have difficulty letting go of certain jobs or responsibilities because they think they are required to be all things to all people. No person can fill that description.

A man who was very good at sales said to me, "I have just been promoted to a regional management position, and I'm struggling." I wasn't surprised. Very often companies make a big mistake in promoting their top salesmen to a staff management position, perhaps in hopes that their top salesmen might teach the gift to those who don't have it. It never works. Salesmen should be left to sell and then promoted or rewarded within a company on the basis of their sales, not their managerial ability.

I said to this supersalesman, "Here's how you can succeed. Hire somebody to handle the day-to-day operations of your department. Find someone who is gifted to be a manager. From what you have told me, the person you need may be a gifted clerical secretary who has some bookkeeping skills."

"But," he said, "the business school I am attending tells me that I can learn to be a good manager."

I said, "If that's the approach you want to take, we shouldn't waste any more of your time or mine. You recognize that you aren't gifted to be a manager. I won't spend time trying to help you become something that God has not gifted you to become."

"What should I do?" he asked. "Should I resign?"

"Not necessarily. Make your calls. Make your sales. Let your selected office manager be the one who runs the office. Reward that person well. You'll both come out ahead. Don't try to become something you are not gifted to be. You'll be miserable, and in the end, you'll make your employees and your family members miserable. Morale will suffer, and your effort will fail. Do what you do well. That will inspire others to do what they are gifted to do to the best of their ability. See what happens."

This man followed my advice, and sales in his region continued to soar, mostly because he was out selling. The person he hired as an office manager had no desire or ability to be in sales. She was very happy running the office, and she was pleased with the rewards she received. This man was actually told by his superiors that he was an *excellent* manager. In actuality, he had made only one management decision—to hire a person to do what he wasn't gifted to do!

Detail thinkers are not global thinkers. Global thinkers are not detail thinkers. We know this intuitively, but when we are faced with a promotion and a greater salary that requires us to do what we are not gifted to do, the temptation is always there.

In the well-known fairy tale of Cinderella, the stepsisters do their best to cram their oversized feet into a glass slipper that was exclusively designed for Cinderella. The person who tries to fill a job when he is not gifted for that job is somewhat like one of Cinderella's stepsisters.

No person is all-purpose. The challenge each of us faces is to find and then to work in close harmony with those who complement our talents and gifts.

LIFE MENTORS

In addition to those who will complement your giftedness, you are wise to seek out those from whom you can learn. These are the people who can help you develop your giftedness and from whom you can receive information, insights, and wisdom to help you grow.

Some dictionaries define *mentor* in very broad terms, such as "coach" or "trainer." That falls far short of my definition. My definition of a *mentor* is this: "wise and trusted adviser, one to whom you can turn for sound counsel."

> ***There are diversities of gifts, but the same Spirit. There are differences of ministries, but the same Lord.*** (1 Cor. 12:4–5)

Types of Mentors

The CEO of one of our nation's largest corporations said to me, "Who can I talk to? If I speak with my wife, she is sympathetic, but she doesn't understand my area of expertise. If I speak with my board, they begin to wonder if they have the right person as CEO. If I speak with my team, they are threatened. They begin to think, *The boss lacks confidence; he is searching*. So I speak with you."

This man regarded me as a mentor, and in his relationship with me, he drew on my experience and expertise to gain new insights into how to resolve the problems he faced in his job. A mentor should always be someone with whom you can talk freely, and who has a solid understanding about what you are saying.

Historical mentors. Every person needs historical mentors. I have several mentors to whom I turn for advice by reading the works that they have left behind or by reading well-researched biographies of their lives. Some of the early church fathers have become mentors to me in recent months. Winston Churchill is a mentor to me. You have a unique privilege to choose from a wide spectrum of people in this age when information about historical figures is so readily available. Choose your mentors wisely!

Living mentors. A person should also have one or two living mentors. If you are a young chief executive officer, for example, your mentor might be a retired CEO who has "seen it all." He would be a vocational mentor to you. If you are in one of the creative arts fields, you might develop a relationship with someone who is truly an outstanding achiever in your particular field.

The Blessing of Spiritual Mentors

I strongly recommend that if you are committed to ongoing spiritual transformation in your life, you find a spiritual mentor. In a family setting, a parent, grandparent, aunt, or uncle may mentor you about how to live life to the fullest in service to God. A spiritual mentor generally functions to help you discover your unique spiritual gifts, which I term *graces.*

No person can be all things to all people. You must never assume in your giftedness that God has given you a set of gifts with which you can impact, benefit, or even communicate adequately with all people. You are given a set of gifts that equip you to meet the needs of the exact people God will send your way for ministry or service. To those people, you will not be all things, but you will provide what is necessary and beneficial.

Just as you are given a selection of God's graces, so you are placed in a body of believers, the whole of which will bear all of the graces necessary for meeting the needs of those in the body. That is God's design for the church—and it works!

A spiritual mentor will help you isolate and name the specific graces that God is manifesting in your life. Such a list can be very affirming. It can also be a constant reminder of your role in the body of Christ. And it can help you stay true to the spiritual calling of God to serve His people.

These graces of God are more clearly manifested, tend to grow more rapidly, and are more brightly reflected in persons who have become "new creatures" in Christ Jesus through their belief in Jesus as the Son of God, and who have an awareness of the Holy Spirit's presence and work in their lives. When you become fully surrendered to God, these graces take on dominance; they find an even fuller expression. They truly become your hallmarks and are a source of inspiration and blessing to others.

Graces reflect the nature of God. Too often, I believe, we limit ourselves in defining or listing the graces of God to traits identified as "fruit of the Spirit" in Galatians 5:22–23—"love, joy, peace, longsuffering, kindness, goodness, faithfulness, gentleness, self-control." While these traits certainly are evidence of the Spirit and are hallmarks of God's character, this list is by no means comprehensive. Indeed, it is only one of several such character-trait lists provided by Paul in his letters.

The graces of God are traits or characteristics that we *always* find in the manifestations of God's nature and that are therefore *always* desirable in all people, in all cultures, at all times. The graces of God are always good, and they are always obtainable in a life surrendered to Christ Jesus. When they are manifested with purity in a person's life, they always bring great blessing and purpose not only to the one who is manifesting them, but also to the person who is the recipient of them.

Growing in the graces. The graces of God are intended to be active in us and through us. They are for using. Thus, to some degree, they are capable of being honed. Anything that has a functional purpose can be developed, improved, or refined.

We *grow* in the graces of God and in our ability to manifest or use them properly. The seed of these graces—usually a unique mix of God's character traits in varying proportions—is in us from birth. The planting, growth, and harvest resulting from the seeds are a lifetime process that takes place, I believe, throughout eternity. We grow in the graces at a considerably faster pace following our surrender to God. The transformation to saintliness is essentially through our spiritual development.

Seeing God's graces in others. When we recognize the presence of the graces of God in others, we have a much greater regard for them and a much greater appreciation for God's love at work in their lives. We are seeing Christ in that person. We truly begin to see others as God sees them—indeed, as God has created them!

For example, in our humanity and from a totally human-nature perspective, we might regard a person as being stubborn and unyielding. We might find such a person difficult to be around and thus regard the person as someone to avoid. If we see this person, however, as having been graced by God with "the strength to remain steadfast and diligent," we will probably have a much greater appreciation for the person, be much more accommodating of that person's actions, and have a greater love for that person. The love of Christ is unconditional. One of the most difficult graces to master in practice is that of offering Christ's unconditional love to all. As we begin to see God at work in others, our hearts toward others are softened. When we surrender, we hunger for the heart of Christ. Offering His love to all becomes our reality.

It is much more beneficial to say to such a person, "I see that God has graced you with the strength to remain steadfast and diligent," than to say to the person, "I think you're stubborn and unyielding." One points toward the positive work of God in the person's life, and it exalts the fact that God has created the person with a unique trait that should be recognized, developed, and used. The other statement denies the work of God in the person's life and undermines the potential for a good expression of a trait God intended for good.

The ultimate spiritual Mentor. Jesus, through the Holy Spirit, is the ultimate Mentor, the Counselor of all believers. As Christians, our foremost concern must be to have an intimate mentoring relationship with our Lord. We must learn to hear His voice continually—guiding us, affirming us, directing us, challenging us, convicting us and, above all, loving us.

How to Find a Mentor

In most cases, you will be able to find a living mentor among your circle of friends, family members, or church members. Look for someone who is about five or ten years your senior, is very trustworthy, has no axes to grind, and is not manipulative.

Give yourself time in finding a mentor. Don't be in a hurry.

Identify what you are looking for in a mentor. As you have gained perspective on your life, you likely have found areas in which you feel that you could benefit from a mentoring relationship. Be absolutely clear to yourself and then to the person you approach as a mentor what you desire out of the relationship.

I recommend the Japanese approach to a mentor. In Japan, the mentor and the mentored have a silent understanding. The Japanese have raised silent understanding to an art form with their oblique, nonfrontal approach. The word *mentor* is never used. Convey your intent, your desire, but don't use the term *mentor*. To do so is to lay a burden on the other party, one that may convey negative images, such as undue responsibility.

After you have identified a mentor and entered into something of a relationship with a mentor, go through a pilot period. If the relationship isn't helpful, gracefully end it. Keep searching. Pray that God will provide for your needs. Believe that He will!

Mentors are for seasons, for periods of time. The only Mentor for life is Jesus. I had a great mentor named Ted Smith, whom I mentioned earlier. When I became dependent on him, he gradually withdrew. After he said on several occasions that he had no idea how to answer a question I posed, I realized the mentoring relationship was over. It was now holding back my growth, and my wise counselor saw it before I did. We continued as great friends. God bless you, Ted, for what you contributed to my life.

LIFEPLAN PARTNER

Having a LifePlan Partner will prove valuable to you. I recommend that this be a friend of your same sex with whom you can confide fully, trust explicitly, and to whom you can be transparent and accountable. You may be wondering if a person could or should have more than one LifePlan Partner at a time. The answer is no. You need only one such person in your life at a time. But you do need that one person. Look at the depth of relationship required as spelled out in the following material. How many people could or would you allow to so speak into your life? God will provide that person. He knows your needs. He fulfills them.

A good LifePlan Partner will know your LifePlan and then will help you to

- be accountable and to keep your promises to yourself.
- think things through.
- encourage you when you need encouragement.
- keep your deepest secrets in confidence.
- help you review your LifePlan periodically and offer suggestions and counsel.

A LifePlan Partner will make himself or herself available to you always, and will count your relationship as a top priority.

My LifePlan Partner and I have met for many years now to hold each other accountable to our LifePlans. He reviews his plan twice a year in an introspective setting and when he returns from what he calls his LifePlan Retreat, he asks me to go over all of his notes. We invest an entire day on this twice a year. He also holds me accountable for my LifePlan. We are LifePlan Partners to each other.

Not a Spouse

I don't recommend that your LifePlan Partner be your spouse. Very often, a person chooses a spouse not for the similarities that exist in their makeup, but for their differences. In many marriages, spouses balance each other, providing a more complete spectrum of emotional, intellectual, and spiritual responses to any one family situation.

Ginny would not enjoy being my LifePlan Partner. Indeed, it would be very upsetting to her, and it would cause us real difficulties. She is problem focused, and the matters I am wrestling with would cause her distress. I'm not saying that your LifePlan Partner absolutely should not be your spouse, but I'd avoid it. Having this relationship with someone else *of your same sex* can result in a very enriching lifelong friendship, a treasure. Why the same sex? Because a man and a woman cannot just be good friends.

Hallmarks of a Good LifePlan Partner

My LifePlan Partner is a dear friend, Gary Liebl, a retired chief executive officer who was my client for more than fifteen years. He knows me well, and I know him well. He embodies what I consider to be the profile of a good LifePlan Partner:

- Practicing Christian
- Close friend of the same sex
- Someone who is "family" to me, in every way a spiritual brother in Christ Jesus and someone who is loved and appreciated by my other family members
- A secure, confident person of wisdom
- Someone who will tell me what I need to be told
- Someone who is a prayer partner
- Someone who will always be there for me; I will never feel as if I am "imposing" on his time by calling him

Do you need to be close geographically? No. But you should try to get together at least once or twice a year. The other criteria are far more important than geographical proximity.

PAUSE FOR REFLECTION

Take a few minutes to reflect on those who have occupied these various roles in your life in the past: persons with complementary gifts, vocational mentors, historical and living "life" mentors, and spiritual mentors.

Identify mentors you may want to add to your life, or relationships with current mentors that you may feel a desire to enhance.

Ask the Holy Spirit to reveal to you the type of wise counsel or complementary assistance that you may need in your life at this time. Ask Him to reveal to you the persons He desires to fill those roles in your life.

Begin to think about person(s) you might contact as a LifePlan Partner.

HELPFUL RELATIONSHIPS

Persons with Complementary Gifts:

Life Domain Mentors:	HISTORICAL	LIVING
PERSONAL		
FAMILY		
CHURCH/ FAITH KINGDOM		
VOCATION		
COMMUNITY		

Possible LifePlan Partners:

Fill in these areas only where needed. If you cannot think of anyone in an area that relates to your life, but you feel you have a need in an area, write "Need" in that space. Make your need a matter of prayer.

13

MODULE #9: PUTTING TOGETHER THE BIG PICTURE

You must actively receive God's plan. You do so by faith. Nevertheless, God's plan does not impact your life fully unless you acknowledge that you are willing to pursue His LifePlan and you yield yourself to it.

A woman said to one of our LifePlan facilitators, "Why did it take God fifty years to reveal to me these things about myself?"

The facilitator replied, "Aren't you glad you know them now?"

"Of course," the woman said. "But there's so little time left for me to use this new information."

"I disagree," the consultant said. "There's all eternity for you to use this new information!"

We err greatly, I believe, in thinking that we will remain who we are at the time of death. God created us for growth, and surely that growth will continue into eternity. We are only at the beginning point of becoming who we will be, the end result of which is unimaginable because none of us can comprehend eternal life, much less what it means to reach perfection. Yet that is what God has promised to give to those of us who are surrendered to Him.

As Paul wrote, "Now we see in a mirror, dimly, but then face to face. Now I know in part, but then I shall know just as I also am known" (1 Cor. 13:12). We see now only the first glimpses of the graces of God at work in us and in others. What a wonder it is to see those glimpses, and yet at the same time, how limited is our view of them. We must recognize that God is the One who is Author, Finisher, Refiner, Developer, Teacher, and Craftsman of our lives. We are His "workmanship, created in Christ Jesus for good works" (Eph. 2:10), and God alone knows fully what means are required to mold us into the people we are to be out of the raw materials that He placed in our lives.

Do all of us bear gifts from God? Yes. We all are created in God's image and therefore bear His likeness and His abilities, some traits being endued more generously than others. We all have the potential to know God, and to grow into His likeness as we yield our spirits to His Spirit. Christ died for all; redemption, therefore, is made available equally to all humankind.

Are all of us aware of God's gifts in our lives? No.

Are all of us growing in the gifts of God in our lives? No, but certainly some are growing in them, and some are growing much more rapidly than others.

Is God at work bringing all of us to an awareness of Himself and of our giftedness? Yes.

Does He desire that we recognize His graces and gifts in the lives of others? Yes.

The answers to these questions come to us through process and over time. We are not birthed with an understanding of how God works, or that we have been gifted by Him. We are all works in progress. That includes our growing awareness and understanding of self, God, and others.

You are not doing fully what you were created to do. You are not fulfilling all of your giftedness exactly as you should be. No one is. But rejoice in this! Don't be dismayed. You have more insight into who you were created to be and what you must do than you had at the outset of reading this book. Furthermore, you have the power and freedom to choose to change, grow, and become increasingly transformed. Your potential is within your grasp. God is wonderful!

SUMMARIZING YOUR PERSPECTIVE

Taken as a whole, your understanding of your life leads you to the point of drawing certain conclusions about life. You can and should state them clearly in a summary fashion for easy review.

Take a look at the Learnings Matrix. It is your working model for summarizing the perspective you have gained. In each box of the matrix, you will be asked to write one or two points of learning that you have gained from the various modules you have completed. The definitions for *life messages, core values,* and *roadblocks to growth* are provided on the next few pages.

LEARNINGS MATRIX

LIFE DOMAINS	LIFE MESSAGES	CORE VALUES	ROADBLOCKS TO GROWTH
PERSONAL			
FAMILY			
CHURCH/ FAITH KINGDOM			
VOCATION			
COMMUNITY			

LIFE MESSAGES

With reference to all of the constructs that you have completed in this book, ask yourself, What is the message to me about the personal domain of my life? The family domain? My vocation? My church/faith kingdom domain? My involvement with my community?

Messages are signals. From an overall appraisal of all the exercises you have completed in seeking a greater perspective on your life, what message comes ringing out to you with clarity?

A Sense of Divine Calling

I often ask the pastors who come to me for help with a LifePlan, "Were you really called to the ministry?" In many cases, the person admits to me after some reflection, "I can't say that I was."

One message that should ring out to you about your life is that you have been called by God to do what He has equipped and created you to do. You should have a strong awareness in any endeavor that you are about the Lord's work and purposes.

What has happened to many people in ministry appears to be this: they felt inside them a desire to serve others, and they assumed that the best way to serve others—or perhaps the only way to serve others—was to enter the pastoral ministry. Being a pastor is a very specific form of service, but it certainly is not the only means of service. And it most certainly is not the right means of service for every person.

We are all called to minister to others. No Christian is exempt from being a minister. The form our ministry takes, however, is unique to our specific calling and to the specific traits, talents, abilities, and desires that God has placed within us and that He has caused to be developed from our birth.

God does not create us and then at some point of maturation, both physical and spiritual, prescribe a means of service for our lives. He creates us with our ministry as part of the plan for our lives from the outset.

The call to ministry is the purpose for our creation initially. What we tend to describe as a call to ministry is actually the moment in which we become aware that God has called us to minister to others. Each of us intuitively knows in that moment of awareness that ministry to others—being of help, service, or blessing to others—is the highest and greatest purpose for our lives and that in serving or ministering, we will experience the greatest fulfillment possible. Why? Because ministry is the reason we exist.

We human beings are the ones who have made a career of ministry. From God's perspective, all of His children are called to be ministers one to another. He refers to the roles of pastors, evangelists, teachers, and so forth as offices within the church. These are prescribed functional roles. But even so, they are the roles designated so that those who are pastors, evangelists, teachers, prophets, and apostles might train and prepare all of the saints under their influence for ministry one to another. (See Eph. 4:11–13.)

Those who come to me for LifePlans and admit, "No, I don't believe I was really called to the ministry," are facing up to the fact that they have been occupying the wrong vocational role or office within the church, not that they do not have a heart for service or a broader call from God upon their lives to use their gifts to serve others.

What about you? Do you have a strong feeling that you were *called* by God to do what you are doing? Do you have a strong awareness that God has ordained you to be His minister—to show His love, express His truth, and be His means of meeting practical needs—to others?

> ***You did not choose Me, but I chose you and appointed you that you should go and bear fruit, and that your fruit should remain.*** **(John 15:16)**

The fact is, all are called. Only some are called to manifest their calling as pastors, teachers, evangelists, prophets, and apostles. Most are called to manifest their calling to ministry in careers or vocations that are not bound to the direct function of the church—as bookkeepers and beekeepers, stewardesses and stew makers, hairdressers and word processors, corporate managers and school janitors. Every career or vocation is a means of ministry, providing both a platform from which to proclaim Christ's gospel in thought, word, and deed, and a congregation of hungry souls who will benefit from the ministry rendered by a loving saint of God.

A Desire for Legacy

One message that you should derive from an appraisal of your life is that we are to leave a legacy to the world. What you do is not solely for yourself. You were created not as an end point, but as a part of an unending plan of God. Legacy flows from what you determine will be the most meaningful contribution of your life.

Lou Holtz, former head football coach at Notre Dame, gave a new meaning to the word *win:* *W*hat's *i*mportant *n*ow? He encouraged his players by telling them that if they could only determine the answer to that question, they would always be winners—not only in football but also in the game of life.

I like to think in terms of the acronym WIL: What's the Important Life? What is the most important contribution you believe you might make to life? What is the most important achievement you can have in life? What is the most important quality you can manifest to others through your life?

Choose to leave a legacy. Make your life count. Make it memorable to others. When you surrender your life to Christ, the Holy Spirit anoints you for His magnificent LifePlan for you—for a legacy beyond anything you could imagine, a legacy that would be overwhelming to you if you were able to envision it.

REAFFIRMATION OF CORE VALUES

What are the "must" rules of your life? What are the rules by which you play the game of life? One person called them the rules of the road. Another person called them bedrock beliefs.

Review the various constructs that you have completed in this book. Look for an expression of values.

Your core values must be what you say you believe in and what you actually practice. You must walk the talk for a value to be a core value.

Your core values are the baseline for all decisions you make. Any decision that is not in keeping with your core values will be unsettling or disconcerting to you. Such a decision will cause you anxiety and stress. In contrast, a decision or action that is in keeping with your core values will be seen as right and, therefore, will bring you a sense of peace, fulfillment, contentment, and joy.

You may find it helpful, as I did, to frame your core values in terms of a contract with God. This is a statement about the values that you choose to reflect in every word, thought, and action. Each person's contract with God will no doubt be expressed in unique terms since each of us is uniquely called to a personal, highly individualized relationship with the Lord Jesus. Nevertheless, the core values expressed by God's Word are central to all believers. God's presence in us and His graces at work through us are common bonds for all surrendered believers.

I offer you my contract only as an example.

My Contract with God

To be
CHRIST-CENTERED

I WILL LIVE BY YOUR **WORD**
coming to know You, Word Incarnate.

I WILL BE GUIDED BY YOUR **SPIRIT**
developing a deep relationship with You, Spirit of Life.

I WILL BUILD MY LIFE UPON YOUR **TRUTH**
because I have given You my heart, Your
truth is in me, God of Truth.

I WILL BE TO ALL A SHINING LIFE OF YOUR **LOVE**
my life being an encouragement, a blessing
to all whom it touches, Love of the World.

And in *all* that I am, *all* that I become, and
all that I do, may it be *all* to Your glory.

Tom Paterson
April 14, 1997

FACING THE ROADBLOCKS

As you review the various constructs of this book, you likely will see roadblocks that are currently standing in your way of future growth.

One person who came for a LifePlan consultation identified the following roadblocks:

- *Personal:* Deep-set need for affirmation
- *Family:* Not trusting enough to be intimate
- *Vocation:* No mentors; not in a situation favorable for growth
- *Church/faith kingdom:* Have not truly surrendered
- *Community:* Not serving my community in any way; job overwhelms all Life Domains

This person found it fairly easy to discern what was going to be necessary for him to grow in his ability to live the life that God meant for him to live. He recognized the next steps that he needed to take.

No Self-Victimization

In identifying roadblocks, some people fall into self-victimization. They perhaps are looking for a means to justify their failures, and they do so by blaming others.

When people get into self-victimization, they invariably close themselves off to an awareness of God at work in their lives. They afford to other people, and sometimes to vague institutions or situations, the power that should rightfully be ascribed to God. Such people are not emotionally ready for a LifePlan or a truthful evaluation of self.

God Is at Work—There Are No Negatives

God is at work in all things—some of which we may perceive to be for our good, other things that we may perceive to be hurtful or negative. The reality, however, is that if God is at work in all things—and if we believe He is always at work to bring us into a deeper relationship with Himself and to transform us more and more into the likeness of Christ Jesus—then we must acknowledge that all circumstances are under God's control. He is using all circumstances to conform us to His will and to train and teach us about His ways, purposes, and plans. He will make good come from all that we experience.

Paul wrote that he was content in whatever situation he found himself. His trust was in "God who raises the dead, who delivered us from so great a death, and does deliver us; in whom we trust that He will still deliver us" (2 Cor. 1:9–10). That certainly didn't mean that Paul liked being in prison or enjoyed being beaten, ridiculed, slandered, or left for dead on a number of occasions. It meant that Paul could and did see God at work in him and through him, no matter the outer environment or situation. He had come to know that the external circumstances of his life were only a means of refining the inner reality of his existence. Therefore, he could endure all things: "I can do all things through Christ who strengthens me." He had come to believe that he ultimately could—and would—benefit from all things: "All things work together for good." Every situation brought Paul to greater strength and power, greater clarity of purpose and focus of ministry, greater witness of Christ's love and plan for humankind. Truly Paul had come to see that God could work *all* things for his eternal good. (See Phil. 4:11–13; Rom. 8:28.)

Opportunities for Change and Growth

Roadblocks should always be perceived as opportunities for growth and change. We are to be content *in* negative situations, not *with* them. We are called to move beyond the negatives. This theme is repeated throughout the New Testament. We are to be overcomers, to endure to the end, to stand against the wiles of the enemy, to be healed, to become whole. Roadblocks exist, but they are rarely insurmountable. Our task is to get over them, around them, or plow through them, trusting the Holy Spirit to do His work in us and in others. As Paul put it, we are more than conquerors! With Christ in us, we cannot fail. I cannot fail! You cannot fail! What a promise that is! And God *always* keeps His promises.

> *None of these things move me; nor do I count my life dear to myself, so that I may finish my race with joy, and the ministry which I received from the Lord Jesus, to testify to the gospel of the grace of God.* (Acts 20:24)

Fear Is Often the Biggest Roadblock

What is the number one thing that keeps us from pursuing or acting on truth? Fear.

I recently read a newspaper article about a major corporation that announced plans to lay off a thousand workers. One of the top executives of this corporation is a friend of mine, a fine Christian man. Several years ago we had a conversation in which he shared with me that he had a desire to leave the company, but he confessed, "I don't know what I'd do."

I said, "Can't you see the trend in your industry and in your corporation?"

He replied, "Yes, but I have a six-figure income and very good stock options."

"Nevertheless," I said, "that isn't going to matter much if this trend continues. If you are going to leave, this is the time to leave. The company is getting into deeper and deeper trouble, you aren't personally in a position where you can effect a correction that will turn things around, and most important, your heart isn't in this position any longer."

He agreed, but he still chose to stay with the company.

This man is only one example that has led me to this conclusion: every decision in life in which reason is not honored is doomed to failure. Fear is one of the enemy's greatest tools.

> ***God has not given us a spirit of fear, but of power and of love and of a sound mind.*** (2 Tim. 1:7)

The godly reasoning process, in my opinion, is one of asking God for a revelation of the truth and requesting from God *the courage and the wisdom* to respond to the truth in His timing and according to His methods. God has given each of us an ability to think through problems and situations. He will reveal to us the truth we need if we are open to receiving that truth, and He will give us the courage required to act on the truth once it is revealed. (See James 1:5.) When we don't move in the direction that truth demands, we make a bad decision or choice.

You will make hundreds, thousands, perhaps even tens of thousands of decisions in your life. When you look back at a decision that turned out to be a bad one that led to failure, frustration, or the building of a wall between yourself and God, you will likely find that you made the decision out of fear. It might have been a fear of loss of income or financial security, a fear of loss of reputation or status, a fear of losing a relationship or the potential for a relationship. Whatever the object of the fear might have been, the motivation behind bad decisions is nearly always fear. In my many discussions along this line, I have never heard of one example to the contrary. The decision driven by fear contravenes one of God's laws. It can be only a bad decision.

This assumes, of course, that you have gone through enough of the reasoning process to have determined what your options were and have thoroughly assessed them.

President Roosevelt was right when he said that we have nothing to fear except fear itself.

LEARNINGS MATRIX

LIFE DOMAINS	LIFE MESSAGES	CORE VALUES	ROADBLOCKS TO GROWTH
PERSONAL			
FAMILY			
CHURCH/ FAITH KINGDOM			
VOCATION			
COMMUNITY			

Taking the Risk

God calls upon you to take risks. Risk is part of the nature of faith; you take a certain risk anytime you trust God. Abraham risked everything in following God's call to "get out of your country, / From your family / And from your father's house, / To a land that I will show you" (Gen. 12:1). His moving away from Haran involved leaving his extended family, friends, business, reputation, traditions, culture, daily routine, established home—virtually everything—to become a wanderer in search of the fulfillment of God's promise to him: "I will make you a great nation; / I will bless you / And make your name great; / And you shall be a blessing" (Gen. 12:2).

Courage is required as you face your Turning Points Profile. Courage is required as you face your giftedness. Courage is required as you move toward a full surrender of your life to God's LifePlan for you.

No Detailed Blueprints

Reason does not require that you know all of the details or all of the specifics related to the future, even to what tomorrow may hold. The end result of reason is not detailed information; rather, the end result of reason is a morally and spiritually sound decision.

A number of people have said to me, "I'll act when I have a certainty in my spirit of what will happen and how things will turn out." The approach that God challenges us to take repeatedly in our lives is this: "Act when you have a certainty in your spirit about what you *should* do, with no other guarantee necessary except the knowing in your spirit that you are doing the right thing in God's eyes." I have found it very helpful in tough decisions to ask myself, What would my Lord Jesus do?

No one is given a twenty-year blueprint for life. That would eliminate all need for daily trust. God did not tell Abraham precisely *how* he was going to be made into a great nation or *how* his name would be great or *what* blessings God would give. Those details were part of the unfolding adventure in Abraham's life.

Frankly I don't think we truly desire to have a twenty-year blueprint. Such information would make life very boring and may actually cause us to live in greater fear or dread. What I see frequently in those who come for LifePlans is a desire for God to provide something better before they are willing to let go of what they presently have. A person, for example, may say, "I'll leave my current position as soon as I land a better job," or "I'll surrender my life fully to God once I have enough in my retirement account."

God seldom offers us any other assurance beyond this: He will be with us, He will lead us, and He will provide for us what is best for us. He will reveal no more than we need to know. He provides for us with *sufficiency*.

Identify Your Learnings

Now record your learnings on the Learnings Matrix. Give yourself sufficient time for reflection. As in all the constructs, aim at breakthrough thinking. Invite the Holy Spirit to lead you into deep spiritual discernment about your life.

What you write here is likely to be the foundation for any plan of action that you choose to develop in response to the new perspective you have gained about your life. An action plan tends to flow naturally from a LifePlan. When you see the main messages of your life, identify the core values by which you choose to live, and isolate and name the roadblocks before you, the next step is to form a plan for developing your gifts, removing the obstacles in your path, and changing your life to reflect the person you truly have been created to be.

A quick review of the basic categories:

- Life messages—these are the broad themes you see for your life. They reflect God's calling for you and what you will leave as a divine legacy.
- Core values—these are the values that you consider to be irrefutable and musts. They are the foundation stones of all you believe and, therefore, all you do.
- Roadblocks—these are the obstacles you see that are keeping you from living out your core values and life messages to the best of your ability.

WHERE GOD POINTS, GOD FULFILLS

A pastor once said to me, "Tom, where the hand of God points, He fulfills."

In illustrating this truth, the good pastor extended his arm and pointed his finger as he said, "Where the hand of God points." He then turned his hand over and opened his hand to reveal his palm as he said, "He fulfills." It was a graphic description I have never forgotten.

What God calls us to do, He provides for us to do. In the course of my facilitating LifePlans, I have discovered that principle to be true without exception.

In Scripture, we have a clear example of this in the life of Paul. Paul required extensive preparation for his life's most important work—the preaching and teaching of the gospel to the Gentile world.

Paul had not intended for that to be his life's purpose. As a zealous Jew, he had initially been vehemently opposed to the young Christian church, persecuting it with violence and witnessing the martyr's death of Stephen. He considered the Jews who were following Jesus to be highly insidious traitors.

After Paul's conversion, he sought to take the gospel to Jews. That was his heart's desire and his intent. Because he was a righteous Jew, the very thought of going outside the Jewish world was not only alien, but repulsive. He had grown up believing the Gentiles were vile, utterly to be avoided, and of little consequence to God. For the most part, Gentiles were regarded as being incapable of redemption. And then, God began to stretch Paul and to reveal to him the greater work for which he had been destined from birth.

As I have studied the life of Paul, I have come to see that from the beginning, God was preparing Paul uniquely for the tasks that lay ahead for him. And as God further refined Paul for that mission in life, He supported Paul fully with His Holy Spirit.

I believe without doubt that this is the same pattern that God has for each one of us—a full preparation for our ultimate purpose in life, a refinement of spirit as we enter into that purpose, and full support as we incarnate His purpose.

Don't hesitate in your pursuit of the changes you see ahead of you. God will be with you as you make them. He will assist you with all of His infinite resources: His wisdom, His strength, His discernment, His courage, His love. And now, one last story as I remember it. . . .

FOUR WORDS TO REMEMBER

A number of years ago, a father took his eight-year-old son, David, to Disneyland. As they stood on the bridge that spans the moat around the Fantasyland Castle, they watched the swans glide silently on the water below. David blurted out one of those blockbuster statements that every parent has experienced at some time, "Dad, I want to talk with the wisest man in the world."

His father said, "Well, that isn't me, Son, but why do you want to do this?" He discovered that his son had learned at Sunday school that very morning about King Solomon. David wanted to learn how to gain wisdom so that he, too, might become as powerful, rich, and famous as Solomon.

Seeking a way out, the father noticed a man standing by Snow White's Wishing Well, not more than twenty feet away. The father noticed that the man seemed pleasant and alone in his musing, so he said to his son, "He might be the wisest man in the world. Ask him! And don't worry, I'll be watching."

David scurried over to the man at the well, stood by him for a few seconds, and then said, "Sir, may I ask you a question? My dad says you might be the wisest man in the world!"

The man looked at David with openness, friendship, and affection. "Well, well, my goodness," he said. "I'm not the wisest man in the world, but tell me, why are you looking for this person?" The boy expressed his intent. The man said, "Perhaps I can be of help. I will give you four words."

Think

"First," the man said, "is *think*. Think about the principles you are going to live by. Principles are rules that will guide you through life. How will you treat others? Will you always give your best effort? Will your words always be strong because they are true? What you believe is important. I'm sure Solomon had his principles, his rules. I have mine. You will need yours to guide you on your journey through life. Think of the rudder of a ship. Your principles are the rudder of the ship of your life."

Dream

"The second word," the man continued, "is *dream*. Dream a big dream in which you play the starring role. The spotlight will be on you. You are the star. What do you intend to do when you grow up? What is it that you'll love doing, that God gave you the talent to do very, very well? That gift becomes the music you were meant to make. It adds a magnificent purpose to your life. Dream a *big* dream!"

Believe

"Third," he said, "*believe,* young David, who seeks wisdom and riches. Believe in yourself. Believe that you are as special as your mom and dad and God all know you to be. Believe in your principles and your dreams. What you believe will be like the wind in your sails, driving you to the distant shore of wisdom."

Dare

"And the final word," the man said, "is *dare*. Dare, David, to develop your dream, your special vision for a good, useful, and great life, a life that will make a difference. Dare to make it happen. Dare to live your dream. It will be a glorious, happy journey. And when you are wise, you'll know that there are many kinds of riches that are far more valuable than money, gold, or jewels."

David listened intently, and he understood all that the man said. He said, "Sir, thank you. I will remember your four words. May I ask your name so I can tell my dad who you are?"

The man smiled and said, "My name is Walter Elias Disney."

I worked very closely with Walt's brother, Roy, and the entire Disney leadership team on the design and implementation of the electronic and information systems of Walt Disney World. The most precious gift I received from that experience was these "four words," which I learned from Mike Vance, the original dean of Disney University. The story is true in all essential details.

Walt Disney remains one of the most famous men that the world of performing arts has ever known. He was committed to family entertainment that was three-dimensional. He dreamed of a theme park, a place of entertainment far beyond the honky-tonk amusement park of his day.

Roy Disney Jr. wrote me that his uncle Walt had wanted "to do something wonderful for the world." He achieved that. He also wrote that his father, Roy Sr., had been very concerned about carrying Walt's dream forward, but he had succeeded in doing that, probably beyond Walt's wildest expectations.

Each of us has something wonderful to contribute to the world. The starting point is to identify not only our giftedness, but also our principles and our dreams. The point at which our talents turn into great success is the point at which we truly dare to act, developing our gifts and turning them into active and loving service for the glory of God.

Choose to *think* God's thoughts about your life.

Choose to *dream* God's dreams about you.

Choose to *believe* God's Word to you and to trust that God is at work in you and through you.

Choose to *dare* to do God's LifePlan.

You won't be disappointed. To the contrary, you will truly come to *live the life you were meant to live!*

A CLOSING PRAYER

Dear God, I love You and Your Son, Jesus Christ, my Savior. My purpose on this earth is clear: to glorify You. I have found myself by inviting Your Holy Spirit to dwell within me. But I do not fully know You; ours is not yet a face-to-face relationship. You have shaped me for Your purpose, but I do not fully know who I am, nor have You fully revealed Your master thought for me. The result is that I am not living the life You meant me to live.

While I have moments of peace, my life is well seasoned with anxiety. I do not know complete peace of soul. I know the reason for my condition: I have withheld from You the gift of my *all*. I now claim, in the name that You place above all names, Jesus Christ, absolute, total surrender: *all* that I am, *all* that I have, and *all* that I can become is Yours.

Grace me with a Christ-centered heart so that my whole being will repose in Your peace, my life becoming a reflection of Your infinite love—a life led by Your Spirit, moment by moment, conforming to Your will. I will live out Your plan for me, in humility, gratitude, dependence, and love.

I gift You with my *all*. Amen.

EPILOGUE

This book has focused on helping you find yourself by finding God in you, and by discovering the gifts that are a sacred trust that God has invested in you. It has been written to help you, a believer in Christ, to know where you are in your spiritual walk. My prayer is that each reader will come to the Christ-centered life of absolute, total surrender.

You may desire to have a professionally facilitated LifePlan conducted by someone who has this mission as a ministry. Such a process very likely will bring you into an even greater awareness of your giftedness and your life's purpose. It is also a process that culminates in the creation of a working plan—an action plan, a response plan—that will carry you from your new levels of self-discernment to very practical application of behaviors in each of the five domains of your life: personal, family, vocation, church/faith kingdom, and community.

The Pathfinders association provides this facilitation.

Over the thirty years that I have been facilitating LifePlans, I have met an increasing number of individuals who—having been through the LifePlanning process—asked me if they might be trained to do such work so that they could help others. In 1996, we organized an association of LifePlanners under the Pathfinders name. Douglas Slaybaugh, a colleague and friend who has been deeply involved in LifePlanning, is president of this association.

LifePlans are facilitated one-on-one, one soul ministering to another soul. A LifePlan consultation takes two days—two very intense days, I hasten to add. Rates vary by facilitator and their position along a path of progressive accreditation.

For information about LifePlanning facilitation, you may write:

Pathfinders
27042 Aldeano Drive
Mission Viejo, CA 92691

NOTES

Chapter 2

1. Mother Teresa, *A Simpler Path* (New York: Ballantine Books, 1995), back cover.
2. "Love Changes Every Thing" from Andrew Lloyd Webber's production *Aspects of Love.* Lyrics by Don Black and Charles Hart, score by Andrew Lloyd Webber.

Chapter 3

1. F. B. Meyer, *Paul—A Servant of Jesus Christ* (Fort Washington, PA: Christian Literature Crusade, 1978), 60.
2. This man is John Baker, a pastor of the Saddleback Valley Community Church in Mission Viejo, California—one of the most watched churches in our nation, with Rick Warren as its founding and senior pastor. Pastor Baker's twelve-step *Celebrate Recovery* process is achieving more than an 80 percent recovery rate for substance abuse. It is a Christ-centered process. You can reach John Baker through Celebrate Recovery Books, 25422 Trabuco Road #105-151, Lake Forest, CA 92630-2797.

Chapter 7

1. Raghu Rai and Navin Chawla, *The Life and Work of Mother Teresa* (Rockport, MA: Element Books, 1996), 19.
2. Arthur Cushman McGiffert, *A History of Christianity in the Apostolic Age* (New York: Charles Scribner's Sons, 1912), 149.